Enhancing Staff Development in Diverse Settings

Victoria J. Marsick, *Editor*
Columbia University

NEW DIRECTIONS FOR CONTINUING EDUCATION

GORDON G. DARKENWALD, *Editor-in-Chief*
Rutgers University

ALAN B. KNOX, *Consulting Editor*
University of Wisconsin

Number 38, Summer 1988

Paperback sourcebooks in
The Jossey-Bass Higher Education Series

Jossey-Bass Inc., Publishers
San Francisco • London

Victoria J. Marsick (ed.).
Enhancing Staff Development in Diverse Settings.
New Directions for Continuing Education, no. 38.
San Francisco: Jossey-Bass, 1988.

New Directions for Continuing Education
Gordon G. Darkenwald, *Editor-in-Chief*
Alan B. Knox, *Consulting Editor*

New Directions for Continuing Education is published quarterly
by Jossey-Bass Inc., Publishers (publication number USPS 493-930).
Second-class postage paid at San Francisco, California, and at
additional mailing offices. POSTMASTER: Send address changes to
Jossey-Bass Inc., Publishers, 350 Sansome Street, San Francisco,
California 94104.

Editorial correspondence should be sent to the Editor-in-Chief,
Gordon G. Darkenwald, Graduate School of Education, Rutgers
University, 10 Seminary Place, New Brunswick, New Jersey 08903.

Library of Congress Catalog Card Number LC 85-644750

International Standard Serial Number ISSN 0195-2242

International Standard Book Number ISBN 1-55542-917-3

Cover art by WILLI BAUM

Manufactured in the United States of America. Printed on acid-free paper.

Ordering Information

The paperback sourcebooks listed below are published quarterly and can be ordered either by subscription or single copy.

Subscriptions cost $48.00 per year for institutions, agencies, and libraries. Individuals can subscribe at the special rate of $36.00 per year *if payment is by personal check.* (Note that the full rate of $48.00 applies if payment is by institutional check, even if the subscription is designated for an individual.) Standing orders are accepted.

Single copies are available at $11.95 when payment accompanies order. (California, New Jersey, New York, and Washington, D.C., residents please include appropriate sales tax.) For billed orders, cost per copy is $11.95 plus postage and handling.

Substantial discounts are offered to organizations and individuals wishing to purchase bulk quantities of Jossey-Bass sourcebooks. Please inquire.

Please note that these prices are for the calendar year 1988 and are subject to change without notice. Also, some titles may be out of print and therefore not available for sale.

To ensure correct and prompt delivery, all orders must give either the *name of an individual* or an *official purchase order number.* Please submit your order as follows:

Subscriptions: specify series and year subscription is to begin.
Single Copies: specify sourcebook code (such as, CE1) and first two words of title.

Mail orders for United States and Possessions, Australia, New Zealand, Canada, Latin America, and Japan to:
    Jossey-Bass Inc., Publishers
    350 Sansome Street
    San Francisco, California 94104

Mail orders for all other parts of the world to:
    Jossey-Bass Limited
    28 Banner Street
    London EC1Y 8QE

New Directions for Continuing Education Series
Gordon G. Darkenwald, *Editor-in-Chief*
Alan B. Knox, *Consulting Editor*

Contents

Editor's Notes

This volume describes strategies for effective staff development. It draws from both the private and the public sectors, but it focuses especially on the latter. Little is known about the common interests of these two sectors. Conversely, little is known about whether staff development models from the public sector could be used in business settings. The authors of this volume illustrate how staff development is highly influenced by its unique context. Nevertheless, some requirements are common to all settings, because organizations are social worlds and dictate many of the priorities of learners.

The Field of Staff Development

The term *staff development* is used loosely at times to refer to many things. In this volume, *staff development* refers primarily to learning strategies, both formal and informal, for the orientation of staff to an organization and for their continued growth and development. People often use *staff development* as a synonym for the narrower field of formal training, or for the much broader field of human resource development (HRD).

The American Society for Training and Development (ASTD), the primary professional association for the field, conducted a study in 1981 (which it is now updating) of HRD and its professionals (McLagan, 1983). The HRD Wheel, used in both studies to define the breadth of the field, includes training and development as one element. Other areas of HRD are organizational development, organization and job design, human resources planning, selection and staffing, personnel research and information systems, compensation and benefits, employee assistance, and union-labor relations (p. 23).

Staff development is provided through private and public organizations and through professional associations, many of which even have their own colleges and offer their own degrees (Eurich, 1985). There have been several attempts to estimate the size and scope of training, primarily in business and industry, but figures vary by report. Carnevale and Goldstein (1983, pp. 32–36) identify some difficulties in arriving at a definitive figure. The surveys themselves are based on different definitions and assumptions and on rather poor data. Training budgets are only one portion of the costs of learning throughout an organization. Estimates include neither activities from nontraining budgets nor such informal learning activities as on-the-job training, supervision and coaching, mentoring, and self-directed learning. Estimates do not always include such

1

indirect costs as maintenance of a training department, trainees' wages, and time spent away from work. Moreover, many companies may underestimate the scope of training, simply because of differences in internal record-keeping systems or because they wish deliberately to downplay costs.

Carnevale and Goldstein also note that a low-end estimate made by Lusterman (1977) for the private sector indicated that companies with five hundred or more employees spent approximately $2 billion on training in 1975. A high-end estimate by Gilbert (1976), based on extending the $1 billion spent by AT&T to other companies, suggested that as much as $100 billion was spent. Craig and Evers's (1981) estimate of $30 billion has been widely accepted as the industry standard, but their figures are also based on the AT&T data, and they use more conservative assumptions because of the smaller scope of training in smaller companies.

ASTD (1986) reports that $210 billion is spent by businesses each year on formal and informal learning, compared to $144 billion spent on elementary and secondary education. These figures are also based on the Craig and Evers (1981) estimate of $30 billion for formal training, with the remaining $180 billion estimated as informal training. An additional $5 billion is estimated for government training. Lusterman (1985) updated his earlier survey, conducted for the Conference Board (Lusterman, 1977), but he focused more on qualitative changes than on estimates of size and scope. He did note, however, that the proportion of employees annually participating in training increased or remained the same more often that it decreased. Clerical staff were least likely to receive training, along with operators and craftsmen, while managers and supervisors received the greatest increases in training.

Every year since 1982, Lakewood Research has conducted a survey of the field that provides insight into both scope and trends in the private sector, despite Lakewood's sample being unequally representative of all organizations by size, sector, and geographic area. More respondents are typically from the manufacturing and financial sectors, from large organizations, and from the Northeast. In 1987 (Lee, 1987, pp. 51–52), the survey indicated that U.S. organizations with fifty or more employees had budgeted $32 billion in that year for formal training. Approximately 38.8 million people in these organizations received formal training, and salespersons received the most. Lusterman (1985) also indicated that managers and professionals benefited from training, while clerical workers were the least well trained, but more than half of all organizations train managers at all levels, as well as clerical workers. Production workers are trained by only one-fourth of the organizations. When type of training is considered, most organizations are seen to provide new-employee orientation, but the greatest emphasis by far appears to be on management, supervisory, and technical skills.

These figures help one appreciate the size and scope of the field, even though they pertain primarily to business. This author could not locate comparable descriptions for the public sector, although their inclusion would expand the already vast figures reported from the private sector. Nevertheless, this volume does not address this quantitative deficiency; it focuses instead on the qualitative trends that can be captured by four key themes: contextual differences between the private and public sectors; change; a focus on learning; and reflection in practice.

Themes

The Private Versus the Public Sector. This volume explores similarities and differences in staff development between the private, for-profit sector and the public (government, voluntary, and nonprofit) sector. A key theme is the ways in which organizational context influences staff development. Drucker (Evangelauf, 1988) notes, with respect to management theory and the nonprofit sector: "It's sufficiently similar so that everything we know . . . can be applied, but sufficiently different so that a good deal of it has to be applied differently" (p. 3). On the other hand, Benveniste (1987, p. xii) notes that for some types of employees, namely professionals, staff knowledge and organizational complexity influence differences more than the profit motive does.

Each chapter of this sourcebook describes staff development strategies in different settings. The last chapter discusses similarities and differences, while still mindful that the same sample presented herein is small and that the examples are not based on empirical investigations.

One of the ills of this field is an overemphasis on technique—as if problems of performance could be resolved so long as one had the right set of tools. Tools are important, but technique must be incorporated into an overall strategy appropriate to organizational context and needs. Both ASTD (1986) and Lusterman (1985) report that "nice to know" courses are increasingly eliminated from programs, and that training is seen as a strategic tool to ensure productivity. In nonprofit organizations, the goals may be different, but the strategic use of staff development is not. Strategy takes into consideration the way in which the organization is structured, how its culture fosters learning, and how systems and the environment interact to influence the nature of this learning.

Change. This theme is explored specifically in Chapter One and reflected in many other chapters. The United States can no longer ignore changes in the world that demand new ways of organizing work and new ways for individuals and organizations to learn, whether in business, colleges, hospitals, or communities. This theme is reflected both in what staff need to know to develop and in how they go about satisfying those needs.

Technology is a key subtheme of change, having created new needs and methods for both working and learning. New products and services are created more quickly through technology, forcing organizations to struggle quickly, continuously, and innovatively to remain competitive. Staff must take on new roles to meet these demands. Furthermore, staff have personally experienced the revolution in technology. Demographically, a new kind of work force is emerging. Many workers are highly educated lifelong learners, and others are considered functionally illiterate. Nevertheless, everyone increasingly depends on technology for communication and decision making. The medium carries the message, creates the demand, and influences the way in which people give and receive information at work and at home.

Learning. Too often, discussions of effective staff training and development are confined to the best ways to deliver formal courses. Unfortunately, the delivery mentality may make trainers more efficient at doing what they know best than at meeting learners' needs. This sourcebook emphasizes learning, defined as the ways in which individuals or groups acquire, interpret, reorganize, change, assimilate, or apply related clusters of information, skills, and feelings. Learning is primary to the way in which people construct meaning in their personal and shared organizational lives. This focus on learning blurs the lines of the classic distinctions, made originally by Nadler (1970), among training, education, and development. Nadler's distinction is based on the purpose of these activities from the point of view of the organization. When the learner's perspective on whether activities are meaningful is primary, this distinction blurs.

Reflection in Practice. Schön (1983, 1987) suggests that practitioners must choose between the high ground of technical rationality (where they scientifically select the best means to solve a problem) and the "swamp" (where most of the challenging, difficult problems lie). It is not always easy to understand problems in the swamp, let alone find and implement solutions, and yet this is the messy reality in which most staff developers live. The gap between swamp and high ground may also account for the difference between injunctions to plan and carry out programs rationally and real programs that rarely follow linear, logical lines.

Schön (1987, pp. 26–29) describes reflection in action as what takes place when spontaneous, routine responses do not produce expected results. People are surprised and react in different ways. Some may stop and think about what went wrong, and others reflect while they are still acting. This kind of reflection has a critical element: People question their assumptions about how things should happen, restructure their strategies, or reformulate the problems. Reflection leads to on-the-spot experiments that may either satisfy the need at hand or lead to more surprises that continue the cycle.

Reflection in action occurs informally among all levels of staff, under the right conditions. Factory workers learn somewhat informally through on-the-job training, professionals may be highly self-directed in keeping up with their fields, and managers chart new territory on the basis of understanding their experience. Cervero (forthcoming) describes the fit between Schön's work and continuing professional education. Nevertheless, little is known about informal learning in organizations. This volume includes some discussion of informal learning and explores its relationship to more structured training, as a way of understanding that relationship and identifying how to use both kinds of learning.

Effective Strategies for Staff Development

Victoria J. Marsick, in Chapter One, examines the need for "training not as usual" in what she sees as a new era for staff development, catalyzed by revolutionary changes of the postindustrial era. She uses three case examples from the private and public sectors to explore the characteristics of an emerging paradigm for the new era: designing for new organizations and for learners. Marsick links informal and formal learning to Schön's concept of reflection in action.

In Chapter Two, Karen Watkins discusses staff development in a research hospital. She introduces the concept of incidental learning, which she defines as learning that is a by-product of accomplishing a task, and relates it to Schön's work on reflection in action. She then examines paradoxes and double binds that perpetuate an environment in which neither hospital staff developers nor their clients can effectively reflect in action. She concludes with implications for the role of incidental learning in staff development.

In Chapter Three, Boyd E. Rossing echoes the theme of change introduced in Chapter One and elaborates on informal learning in his discussion of staff development for volunteers. Rossing draws parallels between the private and public sectors and identifies the modeling function served by the voluntary sector today. Using research on the nature of volunteers' learning, he suggests that ways be found to integrate classroom and on-the-job learning, that staff developers help people learn more effectively from experience, and that learning be supported through job selection, organizational support, and a system of learning relationships and networks.

In Chapter Four, Sandra C. Acebo and Karen Watkins examine trends in faculty development at community colleges. They search for a guiding framework for faculty development, which they see as integrated with personal, professional, organizational, and program development. Acebo and Watkins emphasize informal learning among professionals and an organizational learning system. Using two case studies, they illustrate the way in which assessment has catalyzed an organizationwide, integrated system of faculty development, a system that focuses on learning and involves the entire organization in a communitywide development effort.

One feature of the faculty development efforts described in Chapter Four is learning through action research on one's own practice. This theme is echoed in Chapter Five. Joann Jacullo-Noto describes an action research model of collaboration between higher education and schoolteachers that shows how professionals with different perspectives learn through complex, long-term projects. Jacullo-Noto highlights differences in organizational context and shows the promise this model holds for meeting the challenges in staff development that are currently posed by educational reform movements.

In Chapter Six, Gloria Pierce takes an organizational development perspective on burnout and stress in the social service sector, a phenomenon she sees increasing. She analyzes the unique set of interacting factors that make burnout more likely in social services and then describes a management development strategy for addressing the problem both through training and through the creation of a climate for learning and growth. She concludes with recommendations for staff developers dealing with burnout.

Linda Shatzer, in Chapter Seven, explores the use of technology in training—specifically, a video teleconferencing series introduced in a large corporation. Written from a practitioner's viewpoint, this chapter describes the preparation, delivery, and evaluation of each of five teleconferencing sessions and draws out the lessons learned for other organizations that might wish to experiment with this approach. Shatzer also relates her findings to the small but growing literature on the topic.

Victoria J. Marsick, in the two final chapters, looks at differences in staff development strategies in different types of organizations. She reviews the contributions of the authors of this sourcebook and identifies patterns and implications of their work. She also identifies additional resources for readers who wishes to explore these topics in greater depth.

Victoria J. Marsick
Editor

References

American Society for Training and Development. *Serving the New Corporation.* Washington, D.C.: ASTD Press, 1986.

Benveniste, G. *Professionalizing the Organization: Reducing Bureaucracy to Enhance Effectiveness.* San Francisco: Jossey-Bass, 1987.

Carnevale, A. P., and Goldstein, H. *Employee Training: Its Changing Role and an Analysis of New Data.* Washington, D.C.: ASTD Press, 1983.

Cervero, R. *Effective Practice in Continuing Professional Education.* San Francisco: Jossey-Bass, forthcoming.

Craig, R. L., and Evers, C. "Employees as Educators: The Shadow Education System." In G. G. Gold (ed.), *Business and Higher Education: Toward New Alliances.* New Directions for Experiential Learning, no. 13. San Francisco: Jossey-Bass, 1981.

Eurich, N. *Corporate Classrooms: The Learning Business.* Princeton, N.J.: The Carnegie Foundation for the Advancement of Teaching, 1985.

Evangelauf, J. "The Father of Modern Management Nurtures the Human Element." *Chronicle of Higher Education,* February 10, 1988, p. 3.

Gilbert, T. "Training: The $100 Billion Opportunity." *Training and Development Journal,* 1976, *30* (11), 3-8.

Lee, C. "Where the Training Dollars Go." *Training,* 1987, *24* (10), 51-65.

Lusterman, S. *Education in Industry.* New York: The Conference Board, 1977.

Lusterman, S. *Trends in Corporate Education and Training.* New York: The Conference Board, 1985.

McLagan, P. *Models for Excellence: The Conclusions and Recommendations of the ASTD Training and Development Competency Study.* Washington, D.C.: ASTD Press, 1983.

Nadler, L. *Developing Human Resources.* Houston, Tex.: Gulf Publishing Company, 1970.

Schön, D. *The Reflective Practitioner.* New York: Basic Books, 1983.

Schön, D. A. *Educating the Reflective Practitioner: Toward a New Design for Teaching and Learning in the Professions.* San Francisco: Jossey-Bass, 1987.

Victoria J. Marsick, formerly director of staff training and development for UNICEF, is assistant professor of adult education at Teachers College, Columbia University. Her special area of interest is workplace learning. She is a consultant to the private and the public sectors on staff development and training and is a member of the Institute for Leadership in International Management.

*Organizations today confront revolutionary changes in the
ways they must organize to remain competitive and productive.
Staff developers are keeping abreast and in some cases leading
the way with strategies for helping staff grow and learn.*

A New Era
in Staff Development

Victoria J. Marsick

The Winds of Postindustrial Change

"Business Not as Usual." We are entering a new era in staff development, catalyzed by revolutionary changes in the world of work. The United States is no longer the undisputed trendsetter in business and culture. Perhaps no country can call the shots in quite the same way any more. Ours is an increasingly global economy, with the fortunes of one country intertwined with those of many others through a variety of international, multinational, or binational cooperative arrangements.

Rapid changes in technology and in communications systems have accelerated the pace of doing business, and created a need for "business not as usual," to borrow a term from Mitroff (1987). Mitroff lists the myriad conditions forcing top executives to consider far-reaching changes in their businesses. He believes that organizations will not survive without "(1) clear recognition and understanding of the role that past assumptions have played in operations and (2) continuous experimentation with new organizational forms for introducing and adopting innovations" (p. 90). Thus, some industries are questioning time-honored methods of doing business and changing their structures to meet new demands by experimenting with entrepreneurship and intrapreneurship, decentrali-

V. J. Marsick (ed.). *Enhancing Staff Development in Diverse Settings.*
New Directions for Continuing Education, no. 38. San Francisco: Jossey-Bass, Summer 1988.

zation, networking, participatory management, and the flattening of middle management.

"Training Not as Usual." These changes call for "training not as usual," a direction illustrated by the W. L. Gore company's informal "lattice" system (Bowlesby, 1987). As a member of a task force early in his career, the chief executive officer and founder of Gore discovered that personal interaction was often more effective than the formal chain of command. When he formed his own company, he did away with the organization chart. Employees are called associates, hold no fixed titles or authority, and work on voluntary commitments. Leadership emerges on the basis of "followership."

Associates at W. L. Gore are sponsors, not bosses; they are advocates and role models for others, and they think in terms of how to help others grow and develop. Associates develop their own training plans, assisted by others on their project teams. Other than a few activities, such as orientation to the company's culture and leadership training, few in-house courses are offered. People learn on the job, with the help of sponsors, or go to outside courses. Associates in the organization also offer workshops and seminars after company hours, attended on a voluntary basis.

Changes in the work force support an argument for "training not as usual," in part because employees are becoming more educated and jobs more sophisticated. It is clear that professionals have to run just to keep pace with the information explosion. Many unskilled workers require remedial education to perform their work, in part because of the large influx of immigrants. Feuer (1987) concludes, through a review of recent studies on the demographics of the work force and new job requirements, that jobs are generally becoming more complex and require higher levels of cognitive skill. Workers in all types of organizations need a broader repertoire of skills than before and, to remain motivated, want a greater stake in the company's success.

This chapter explores the implications of these changes for staff development.

Examples of New Directions

The first example, drawn from local government, shows how management and labor have combined training, informal learning, and other systematic changes to improve productivity, build new cultural norms, and enhance the quality of work life. The second example, drawn from a private consulting group, shows how drama, marketing, and learner-centered principles enliven training for a service orientation. The final example, drawn from a consortium to develop leadership in international management, illustrates Mitroff's (1987) exhortation to question old assumptions and actively experiment with new forms of formulating and resolving problems.

Creating a Culture of Learning. "The 1980s have seen New York City's Department of Sanitation emerge as a paradigm for improved productivity and organization effectiveness" (Timpone and Sussman, 1988). The authors chronicle the role that training has played in this success, along with other critical inputs: gainsharing, labor-management committees, improved labor-management communications, and new technology. A human development division, established in 1984–1985, introduced a pilot "excellence" program. Based on a packaged training program modeled after the work of Peters and Waterman (1984), the training was adapted internally and made available to the department's approximately 1,300 first- and second-line supervisors. Training had to address the following points (Timpone and Sussman, 1988).

- Training would have to allow people to think and contribute, following up with field facilitation and allowing participants a chance to be heard.
- A process was needed whereby people could work through and combat feelings of alienation.
- Management would have to share reasons why the organization was in the state it was and why past decisions were made and strategies formulated.
- Participants must be allowed to actually confront the unseen internal bureaucracy rather than to blame their inability to get things done on the elusive "them" [p. 108].

To meet these needs, the training was designed in two-day units for eleven class days over six months. Classes departed from the traditional lecture format in favor of facilitated group discussion. Each two-day session ended with an action-planning workshop, followed by field visits to assist trainees in resolving problems on site. The next session began with a debriefing on progress and problems, before a new topic was introduced. Facilitators were trained to refrain from giving expert advice and instead to give trainees the power to define and resolve problems. Discussion was not constrained, gripes were aired, and hot issues were debated without punishment or reprisal. Trainees could see for themselves that the organization wanted to change the order of doing business and that they were being asked to define directions, set goals, innovate, and take risks. They could also see that they would be rewarded for their efforts.

Participants have been encouraged to bring work problems into the classroom and take learning back to the job. Training is not being replaced by informal learning, but a new relationship is emerging between the two, illustrated by the establishment of peer networks, in which workers are identified who have been "ready, willing, and proficient in helping their coworkers" (p. 112). These networks foster informal learning on the job.

In essence, this program is creating a climate for learning that goes beyond the classroom. Timpone and Sussman discuss reasons for the program's success. First, the program has the backing of top management and union leaders, who also participate in training sessions. Second, training began at the top but was moved downward to the field officers and the sanitation workers they supervised. Third, the program facilitated participation across traditionally hierarchical lines. Fourth, through a network of teams, the program involved many key stakeholders in design, implementation, and follow-up. The diverse design team included supervisors, a project manager from the labor-management committee, a consultant in participative management, and an experienced program developer and evaluator.

Training for a Service Orientation. The M. Price Corporation, a private consulting group, used training to support its service orientation. In sectors such as banks and high technology, the "quick sell" is being replaced by consultative selling, which places a premium on a continuing relationship with clients (Webster, 1987). Sales training is changing to meet this and other needs (Del Gaizo, 1987), and by some reports, is gaining in importance (Lee, 1987, p. 52). Organizations are also increasing their customer-service training, a development that indicates greater sensitivity to the service orientation.

Nevertheless, most organizations still tend to treat sales and customer-service training separately. The M. Price Company believes that customer relations is good business, not only for sales but also for many other functions. For example, problems often arise when a manager does not understand his or her own "customers," the employees. Price trains people to understand customers and put their needs first. A service orientation with customers also means a service orientation with employees; staff do unto others as is done unto them, a stance that implies changes in training strategies, and in the organization's systems, to support new behaviors.

The M. Price Corporation works with and responds to change by developing customized training programs for employees and program events for consumers. For example, the consulting group helps banks determine what they must do differently in order to attract the women's market. Price designs both a marketing package to meet women's needs and an internal training package that helps bank staff and managers interact differently with their customers. Products often serve multiple purposes; for example, the same video might be used both in staff training and with customers. The training package models principles basic to a service orientation. Thus, staff members are treated as if they were clients. Trainers are continually sensitive to staff needs and are always prepared to depart from their scripts if the situation calls for it. Key ideas do not vary, but objectives may be met differently for each group. These interventions touch deeply on aspects of the organization's culture that support desired behaviors.

An assumption of this approach is that people learn best when they enjoy the process. Training is therefore designed to be both entertaining and instructional. Price's training often incorporates role playing, built around actual problems to ensure relevance. These miniature case studies can be videotaped, packaged, and reused by the company in further training. Role playing reenacts a situation but does not provide a standard, prescriptive solution. It prompts creativity while helping each person try out new skills.

Questioning Assumptions and Creating Experiments. The Management Institute in Lund (MiL), Sweden, designed a strategy similar to an approach called action learning, used by Revans in England during the 1950s (Pedler, 1983; Revans, 1971). Revans observed that people learn best from and with others while tackling real-life problems. He found that, under the right conditions, learners developed "questioning (Q) insight" from their experience, rather than relying on expert "programmed" (P) knowledge unsuited to their needs. Action learning is designed to foster "Q" learning through a group-facilitated cycle of action and reflection. "P" learning is added only after the learners are sure they need this knowledge and know how they will use it. Action learning assumes that people learn best when they examine their own experience, are involved in real problems, and face new situations (Foy, 1977, pp. 158–159).

MiL developed its model by working with some thirty Swedish companies over the last eight years. Each program typically takes place for thirty to forty days over an eight to twelve month period. The core of MiL's program is work in project teams on actual company problems. Managers usually work on problems in different companies and different areas of expertise from their own. Teams consist of three to four people, with no more than one member from the same company or department on each team. Each team represents a broad mix of perspectives and backgrounds. The work and learning of each project team is supported by a project facilitator and supplemented by activities, in small or larger groups, related to project work, personal growth, or management issues.

Facilitators help managers reflect on their experience, become aware of and challenge assumptions, and learn about the dynamics of their groups. Peers and leading thinkers who are invited as resources bring multiple perspectives that help groups reformulate the problems. Managers thus learn from real-life conditions that include complex problems; teams working under time pressure, when members often do not know each other well; multiple stakeholders and sets of social norms and values; unclear goals; and incomplete information.

An Emerging Paradigm for the New Era

Marsick (1987; forthcoming) describes an emerging paradigm, which she contrasts with current models. These are characterized by Goldstein (1980) as behavioristic. Staff development is currently governed primarily by the organizational ideal of a well-functioning machine with clear heirarchical lines of authority, jobs that do not overlap, and rational systems of delegation and control. Training is designed to fill individual deficits, so that workers measure up to standard, expert-driven norms. Training is oriented to behavioral outcomes that can be observed, quantified, and criterion-referenced.

In current models, personal and work-related development are separated. The current ideal is a practical problem-solving aproach that emphasizes objectivity, rationality, and step-by-step procedures. Training typically consists of classroom-based, formal group activities. While trainers recognize the importance of the environment, they often feel they have little control over it and therefore focus on "pure" learning problems. If they can, they build in mechanisms to help individuals transfer learning back to the job and to manipulate the environment to sustain outcomes.

Marsick suggests that the current approach works well under many conditions but that a new paradigm of "training not as usual" is emerging. People are being trained for new kinds of organizations, using new training designs that combine formal and informal learning and include a questioning of old assumptions.

New Kinds of Organizations. Timpone and Sussman (1988) describe New York City's Department of Sanitation as a "quasi-military-type structured environment where change was always suspect" (p. 108). Even here, however, the organization is struggling to develop a team effort, with mechanisms for lateral interaction across boundaries. Our second example, training by the M. Price Corporation, must be viewed in the context of a trend in business toward a service orientation. Carlzon (1987), who turned Scandinavian Airlines around with a service approach, explains that service requires "flattening the pyramid" between customers and top management. Carlzon made his first-line field staff the experts. He decentralized operations and broadened the jobs of employees, so that they could step in and perform a variety of services. Training for a service orientation prepares people for more autonomy, creativity, judgment, and participation in decision making. MiL, the source of our third example, develops managers who question assumptions, communicate across organizational boundaries, decentralize, work in teams, and encourage more autonomy in staff.

Training Designs That Transcend Behaviorism. Workplace learning should help people act differently and improve productivity, and the prevailing behavioral models of instructional design have made progress toward that goal in many cases. When there is one right answer to a problem, and when that answer calls for unswerving reliance on a single expert-based solution, behavioral models work. Behavioral models also serve other needs. They promote uniformity of action, clarify what learners need to do to satisfy employers' needs, make learning manageable by focusing on specific objectives, and uphold minimum organizational standards.

The problem is not that behaviorally based models are used, but that they prevail when conditions call for other approaches. These conditions include situations in which neither problems nor solutions are clear, routine responses do not work, judgments are required that cannot be reduced to simple sets of rules, technique is mediated by unpredictable human interactions, and workers are asked to use their experience and education to anticipate problems and respond creatively.

Models such as those described in this chapter recognize that behavioral change is influenced by complex personal and social norms, in addition to expert-based, task-oriented information. In the Department of Sanitation example, behavioral skills were taught, but equal time was also given to helping employees explore the norms encouraged by the culture of the organization. In the service-training example, the focus was on getting people to think differently about the people they served. The M. Price Corporation did this by helping staff gain insight into themselves and their own communication patterns. Trainees then used these insights to stretch themselves and experiment with new responses. The third example also went beyond predefined behavioral objectives. A key focus of MiL's program was insight into oneself as a member of a work team, a family, and a community, and into one's organizational culture. It quickly became clear that most problems were not "out there" in the land of technical solutions; the knottiest problems faced by organizations are people problems. As group members evaluated problems, they frequently found that the real difficulty was the personality of a key manager or a key team member, or perhaps even their own personalities. This emphasis on self-insight represents a movement away from the separation of personal and professional development. In this example, personal development was not considered to be separate from the job, antagonistic to it, or merely supplementary to it. People were seen to learn best about their jobs when their own identity and growth were recognized as integral to their learning.

All three examples emphasized teamwork, an emphasis not in itself unusual, but they also emphasized team training to build habits that will continue on the job. This emphasis was strongest in the MiL example, with a model built around project teams. All three organizations also created learning communities that they wanted to extend through networking and informal learning back on the job. The success of this feature depends on the commitment of the organization. The Department of Sanitation, for example, has created networks and identifies people who are willing to teach others informally. Graduates of MiL continue to meet regularly, sometimes collaborate on projects outside their companies, and often create learning communities in their own work units.

Questioning of Old Assumptions. The final feature of this new paradigm is the questioning of old assumptions and experimentation with new ones. The clearest example of this feature is offered by MiL, whose programs are designed to move managers out of familiar habits and environments, almost as though they were taking a trip to another country, and to enable them to see situations from new perspectives and question their automatic judgments about the nature of a problem and how it should be solved. While the Department of Sanitation does not go this far in its program, it does illustrate an organizationwide effort to bring many taken-for-granted beliefs, attitudes, and practices to light and revamp them. The M. Price programs, while implemented differently in each organization, encourage individuals to ask questions about themselves and their interactions with others.

Implications for Staff Developers

McLagan (1986, pp. 2–4) suggests that in today's information age, judgment is more important than standardization. New technology and accelerated change demand competitive positioning, which in turn demands greater participation in decentralized decision making, anticipation of problems before they happen, integration across functions and levels, and creativity at all levels. McLagan suggests that "structured and self-managed development become the norm" (p. 8) for managers. In other words, managers must take responsibility for their own learning (as illustrated in the W. L. Gore example), using many nontraditional resources: "films, videos, cassettes, courses, trade and professional association meetings, peers, on-the-job experiences, participation in meetings, special assignments and rotations, journals, reports, close-circuit and cable programs, books, computer-aided learning, programs designed to promote self-discovery, and more" (p. 9). For this effort to be effective, the organization must support and reward learning and integrate it with other human resources practices.

McLagan's suggestions are echoed by Honeywell (1981) and McCauley (1986). Their focus is on managers, but staff development for all employees should be reassessed, to help them learn better from and through their experience. This goal means an enhanced role for informal learning and a new look at its articulation with training. The following suggestions amplify these points.

Designing to Support the New Organization. Various authors use the image of a hologram, the laser-created photograph in which the whole can be reproduced from any part, to describe the new organization (Mitroff and Kilmann, 1984; Morgan 1986). Taken to extremes, this approach could be chaotic, but on a smaller scale, it means that employees at many levels should learn many aspects of the business, rather than being confined to one small, routine part, so that they can more actively anticipate and solve problems.

The unit for coordinating this broader range of talents should be a new kind of team. Teams in the past have primarily ensured that each person plays a well-defined role in carrying out goals set at a higher level of the hierarchy. Teams in the future must be more like orchestras, to borrow a metaphor from the M. Price Corporation. Each person contributes his or her talents more creatively, from start to finish of a project. Some clarity of role definition is sacrificed, but the final product is usually better. There are two caveats, however. First, many employees may not be ready for what may seem to be a lack of structure. This kind of teamwork requires self-discipline, tolerance for ambiguity, and a willingness to submerge one's own needs to the group's goals. Second, there are times when routine procedures need to be performed efficiently; teams then work best when roles and tasks are clearly delineated and hierarchically managed.

Staff developers cannot change an organization by themselves, but they can work with top management to change policies to this end and can promote job rotation, job enhancement, work redesign, and training to facilitate these changes. A change in corporate culture may be necessary, such as that undertaken at the New York Department of Sanitation. General Electric (GE) provides an example of the use of training to orient staff to a culture change, to teach key skills, and to introduce risk taking, experimentation, innovation, and teamwork (Lusterman, 1985, pp. 3-4). At GE, training is related to problems on the job, which are brought into the classroom. Outdoor challenges, such as rafting, are combined with case studies and teamwork on actual business problems (see "GE's Training Camp," 1987).

Designing to the Learner. Trainers often judge themselves, and may be judged, by the number of courses they conduct, the number of trainees, or the number of satisfied users, as indicated by highly positive workshop evaluations. By contrast, employees benefit most from training when it meets a current need, not a training schedule. As the Department of Sanitation example illustrates, networks of colleagues and supervisors can help one another learn—often informally, through discussions in the hall—when problems and challenges arise.

How can staff developers enhance informal learning, particularly when it is possible to destroy its value by overformalizing it? Honeywell (1981) has turned to steps that include making training more relevant and accessible, establishing a network of people who can serve as coaches and mentors, increasing managerial responsibility for subordinates' learning through job experiences and trial and error, and designing organizational incentives and rewards for learning. One of the designers of Honeywell's approach explained in a seminar that managers seek training for basic skills but that, once these are mastered, they want help with assessment and opportunities for self-development.

Training should not be eliminated; it should be redesigned to complement and facilitate learning through experience. Kolb's (1984) experiential learning theory, while critiqued by some as too simplistic (Jarvis, 1987), helps the trainer in the classroom understand the learner and use experience as a basis for teaching (Kolb and Lewis, 1986). Kolb suggests that people apprehend and transform their experience differently. Some apprehend through concrete experience; others, through abstract conceptualization. Some transform through reflective observation; others, through active experimentation. On the one hand, people tend to have different styles of learning, based on some combination of these dimensions; on the other, their learning tends to follow a cycle that moves from experiencing to observing to conceptualizing to experimenting and back to experiencing. Kolb's work helps trainers understand learning styles, their own and their trainees'. While not slavishly following the learning cycle, trainers know that it is better to help learners understand the meaning of their experience before drawing generalizations, translating theory into practice, and trying out new behaviors. Kolb has also linked his work with the way people think in different professions and occupations, enabling trainers to adapt learning to the ways trainees in different jobs may think because of their work.

All three organizations used as examples in this chapter build learning around experience. The M. Price Corporation does this through projective dramas and minicases taken from company situations. MiL's program has the advantage of an extended time frame in which people work on real-life projects, so that trust can be built within groups, a wide range of job issues can be examined, and experiments can be undertaken with consequences from which the group also learns. The Department of Sanitation plans for action, helps people implement on site, and then examines consequences in the next class period. It is not just that experience is incorporated into the learning design; many training designs include simulations, practice exercises, role plays, and case studies. Rather, the difference in these examples is that participants' experience is the starting point for learning, and that experience in the workplace and learning are directly linked through training. Experience

Figure 1. Adaptation of Kolb's Experiential Learning Cycle

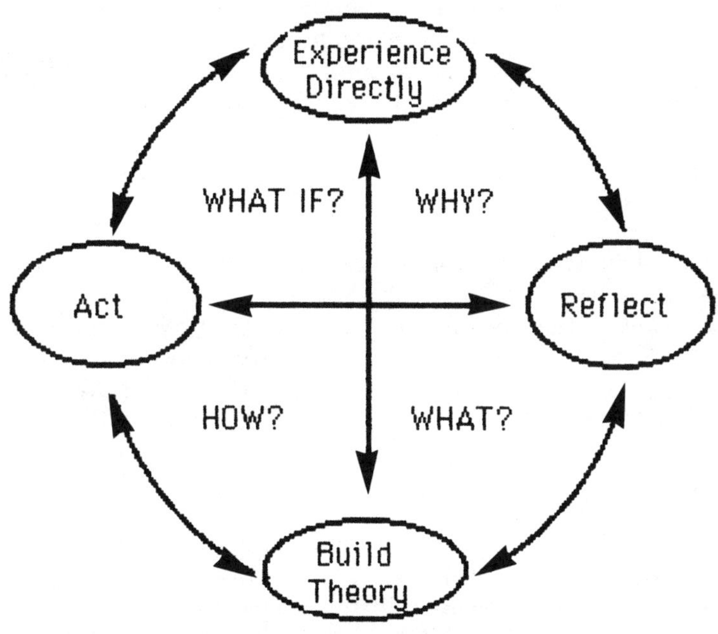

Source: Institute for Leadership in International Management, 1988.

is not provided primarily to practice or illustrate a theory introduced by outside experts.

Staff of the Institute for Leadership in International Management, a consortium now being established in New York and modeled on MiL, have worked with McCarthy (1987) to adapt Kolb's experiential learning theory to describe what takes place in action learning programs (Figure 1). While all elements of the cycle take place in action learning, the emphasis is on people building their own theories, rather than on their understanding and practicing theories developed by others. The focus is on the learner as actor. Therefore, the model primarily helps people actively experiment, directly experience the consequences of their actions, and reflect on the situation. Only then do learners spend time on conceptualizing the theories they may be developing, determining their theories' "fit" with other theories, and deciding if and how the new approaches should be recreated. In this way, action learning is more concerned with what McCarthy (1987) calls the "why" and the "what if" than with the "what" and the "how."

Marsick (1987, forthcoming) suggests that training in today's post-industrial era helps employees develop what Schön (1983, 1987) calls reflection in action. Staff development can build skills in exploring and naming the problem before rushing to solve it and in examining errors critically, even when this means naming the undiscussable and airing old assumptions. The action learning example in this chapter illustrates this process of reflection in action. In action learning, peers learn from peers, while the trainer prompts them to think from different viewpoints and holds a mirror to their actions.

Conclusion

Changes in this postindustrial era are forcing people to rethink their goals, their strategies for working, and the ways in which they organize themselves to accomplish these new aims. This chapter has examined some of the innovations being used to reshape staff development as it enters the new era. Change can be disruptive; but, for some organizations, these times offer challenging opportunities for "training not as usual."

References

Bowlesby, J. "The Great Debate: Training Versus Collaborative Learning." Presentation at the New York Metropolitan Chapter, American Society for Training and Development, December 7, 1987.

Carlzon, J. *Moments of Truth.* Cambridge, Mass.: Ballinger, 1987.

Del Gaizo, E. "Sales Training: Changing Roles, Changing Needs." *Training and Development Journal*, 1987, *41* (5), 46–47.

Feuer, D. "The Skill Gap: America's Crisis of Competence." *Training*, 1987, *24* (12), 27–35.

Foy, N. "Action Learning Comes to Industry." *Harvard Business Review*, 1977, *55* (5), 158–168.

"GE's Training Camp: An 'Outward Bound' for Managers." *Business Week*, December 14, 1987, p. 98.

Goldstein, I. L. "Training in Work Organizations." *Annual Review of Psychology*, 1980, *31*, 229–272.

Honeywell Corporate Human Resources and Employee Relations. *Honeywell Management Development Survey.* Minneapolis, Minn.: Honeywell, 1981.

Institute for Leadership in International Management. Unpublished diagram, New York, 1988.

Jarvis, P. "Meaningful and Meaningless Experience: Towards an Analysis of Learning from Life." *Adult Education Quarterly*, 1987, *37* (3), 164–172.

Kolb, D. A. *Experiential Learning.* Englewood Cliffs, N.J.: Prentice-Hall, 1984.

Kolb, D. A., and Lewis, L. H. "Facilitating Experiential Learning: Observations and Reflections." In L. H. Lewis (ed.), *Experiential and Simulation Techniques for Teaching Adults.* New Directions for Continuing Education, no. 30. San Francisco: Jossey-Bass, 1986.

Lee, C. "Where the Training Dollars Go." *Training*, 1987, *24* (10), 51–65.

Lusterman, S. *Trends in Corporate Education and Training.* New York: The Conference Board, 1985.

McCarthy, B. *The 4 Mat System.* Barrington, Ill.: EXCEL, 1987.

McCauley, C. D. *Developmental Experiences in Managerial Work: A Literature Review.* Greensboro, N.C.: Center for Creative Leadership, 1986.

McLagan, P. *Strategic Management Development.* St. Paul, Minn.: McLagan & Associates, 1986.

Marsick, V. J. (ed.). *Learning in the Workplace.* Beckenham, Kent, England: Croom-Helm, 1987.

Marsick, V. J. "Learning in the Workplace: The Case for Reflectivity and Critical Reflectivity." *Adult Education Quarterly,* forthcoming.

Mitroff, I. I. *Business Not as Usual: Rethinking Our Individual, Corporate, and Industrial Strategies, for Global Competition.* San Francisco: Jossey-Bass, 1987.

Mitroff, I. I., and Kilmann, R. H. *Corporate Tragedies: Product Tampering, Sabotage, and Other Catastrophes.* New York: Praeger, 1984.

Morgan, G. *Images of Organization.* Newbury Park, Calif.: Sage, 1986.

Pedler, M. *Action Learning in Practice.* Aldershot, Hants, England: Gower, 1983.

Peters, T., and Waterman, R. H. *In Search of Excellence.* New York: Warner Books, 1984.

Revans, R. W. *Developing Effective Managers: A New Approach to Business Education.* New York: Praeger, 1971.

Schön, D. *The Reflective Practitioner.* New York: Basic Books, 1983.

Schön, D. *Educating the Reflective Practitioner: Toward a New Design for Teaching and Learning in the Profession.* San Francisco: Jossey-Bass, 1987.

Timpone, J. J., and Sussman, P. E. "Excellence Training for Productivity." *Public Productivity Review,* 1988, *11* (3), 105–115.

Webster, B. *The Power of Consultative Selling.* Englewood Cliffs, N.J.: Prentice-Hall, 1987.

*Victoria J. Marsick, formerly director of staff training and
development for UNICEF, is assistant professor of adult
education at Teachers College, Columbia University. Her
special area of interest is workplace learning. She is a
consultant to the private and the public sectors on staff
development and training and is a member of the Institute
for Leadership in International Management.*

*Staff development in the complex, turbulent environment of
a research hospital may be undermined by counterproductive,
tacit learning norms that allow no critical reflection on
practice.*

Paradoxes of Staff Development in a Research Hospital

Karen Watkins

The case study on which this chapter is based is of a research hospital in
Texas with a number of unique characteristics. Imagine having only two
weeks to train the support personnel for a surgical team about to implant
a new version of a mechanical organ, when you have never seen the
device, or being asked to design a chemical safety training program that
meets new federal regulations for over 2,500 people, with less than a
month's lead time. In these examples, there is an emergency-room climate—a sense of urgency and of life-threatening consequences for any
mistakes. Moreover, staff development in this setting is also unique in
that, although continuing education is not mandatory by state law, it is
by this hospital's policies. Staff development is conducted under demanding conditions by committed, dedicated professionals.

Hospital staff development must answer to many masters. Every
health care specialization has specific guidelines framed by its professional association. State licensing boards, accreditation agencies, and
local hospital policies may all also specify the nature of staff development
needed by specialty. The field of health care is in considerable upheaval,
as diagnostic-related group payment schedules, a critical nurse shortage,

V. J. Marsick (ed.). *Enhancing Staff Development in Diverse Settings.*
New Directions for Continuing Education, no. 38. San Francisco: Jossey-Bass, Summer 1988.

exponential technological growth, and a major catastrophic communicable illness—AIDS—all begin to upset "business as usual." These changes have produced not only a need for education for hospital staff but also a changed organizational culture.

Moccia (1987) notes that the health care delivery system is fragmented, alienating, and dehumanizing for patients and nurses alike. She identifies a contradiction between a mission to care for others and a system that seems to obstruct that mission. Del Bueno and Freund (1986) comment that the concept of organizational culture allows us to go beyond the mechanistic or instrumental view of the organization to the symbolic and expressive aspects. It is at this level that the contradiction can be seen. The culture of the hospital is complex, nonroutine, and often ambiguous or contradictory. Under these conditions, a critical reflection on the assumptions and an examination of the paradoxes implicit in managing these changes will enable hospital staff developers to design their own and others' learning cultures more proactively.

This chapter reports a case study of one research hospital's staff developers' paradoxes and double binds. The chapter begins with a review of various definitions of hospital staff development, with special emphasis on nursing staff development, since the sample was drawn largely from nurse educators. Nonformal approaches to nurse education, and the potential of action learning and reflection in action as alternative forms of staff development, are emphasized. These forms enable staff developers to work at the expressive level of the organization. The paradoxes observed among one group of health care educators, and the contradictions between the espoused mission of staff development and actual practice, are described and illustrated. Finally, implications for hospital staff developers are put forth.

Defining Staff Development for Nurses

Continuing Education. Continuing education for nurses helps "to enhance their competence in their work role" (Clark, 1979). The American Nursing Association (ANA) defines continuing nursing education as "planned, organized learning experiences designed to augment the knowledge, skills, and attitudes of registered nurses for the enhancement of nursing practice, education, administration, and research, thus improving the health care of the public" (Cooper, 1983). Cooper also distinguishes among continuing education, inservice education, and staff development. Inservice education is a training program offered by an employing agency, while staff development is a much broader term, since it includes both formal and informal learning opportunities and encompasses the total development process. Staff development, in this sense, is consistent with the American Nursing Association's definition, which includes orientation, inservice education, and continuing education but it is also more inclusive, since it picks up informal learning. For O'Connor (1986), the ANA definition implies that staff development will be related to performance expectations in the work setting. According to Tobin, Wise, and Hull (1979),

> A distinctive aspect of in-service education is incidental learning, which refers to potential learning situations that may or may not be planned efforts but that contribute significantly to an individual's continued development. It is this aspect of staff development that has the greatest potential to capture that teachable moment. A frequent example of incidental learning is physician-nurse conferences relating to a patient. During such an exchange, the nurse may reveal new research data relating to the teaching process for comparable patients and the physician may share new research data relating to the patient's pathological conditions. Neither *planned* to learn these new items; the learning occurred *incidentally* to the planned event (a patient conference) [p. 9].

Incidental Learning. Incidental learning is the focus of this chapter. Incidental learning has been defined as "learning which is a by-product of accomplishing a task" (Watkins and Wiswell, 1987). Nadler (1982) sees incidental learning as learning from experience, from living and adapting to our environment. For him, this learning interacts with intentional learning and results in performance. Nevertheless, incidental learning lacks design, is often not discussed, and, because it is seldom analyzed, potentially has a higher incidence of error than other forms of learning (Watkins and Wiswell, 1987; Argyris and Schön, 1978). Some form of critical reflection must transform or interpret experience in such a way that the individual learns and changes his or her knowledge or practice, rather than simply repeating an error.

Levitt and March (1987) note that both trial-and-error learning and incremental search (learning that represents a series of successive approximations) depend on whether individuals interpret the outcomes of learning activities as successes or failures. Individuals tend to reinterpret results so that they can claim them as successes. At the organizational level, political processes may lead to frustration, as individuals' aspirations exceed reality and as conflict during implementation reduces the likelihood of success. Incidental learning includes learning by doing and learning from actions framed as mistakes, and so determining the meaning that individuals attribute to learning experiences becomes critical to examining the biases inherent in such learning.

Argyris and Schön's (1978) theory of organizational learning postulates that individuals act as agents for the organization; thus, one can determine the overall learning norms of an organization by aggregating those of individuals. They also observe, however, that people often espouse theories that are belied by action, and that they seldom examine these contradictions; thus, people create, maintain, and sustain dysfunctional organizational norms that become undiscussable. Staff and their organizations come to live with double binds or paradoxes, and individuals and their organizations become less able to learn and be productive. These undiscussable norms are often learned incidentally and transmitted unconsciously by an organization's members, including those most responsible for learning in the organizations—the staff developers.

Watkins and Wiswell (1987) studied the learning practices and learning norms of hospital staff developers, using Argyris and Schön's work as a theoretical framework. The binds and themes they identified may have implications for the improvement of hospital-based staff development programs.

Studying Staff Developers in a Research Hospital

The hospital that furnishes the example for this case study is very large and enjoys an international reputation for its research. At one time, over eighty people in various departments throughout the hospital had staff development responsibilities. Many of these people had no idea of what the others were doing, and so the hospital centralized the staff development function into one large education department and hired a new high-level administrator to manage it. Morale, which had been high when this change took place, steadily dropped; one key administrative slot remained unfilled for over a year, and all leadership roles remained on an "acting" basis. As part of this transition, a redefinition of the department's mission and a reorganization of its structure were undertaken.

The case study described how staff developers themselves learned, and how their learning compared with how they helped others learn. On the basis of the work of Argyris and Schön (1978), Watkins and Wiswell (1987) expected to find gaps between espoused learning norms and actual practice. In all, eighteen individuals (about 25 percent of the total population) were each interviewed for an hour about how they had last learned something to solve problems in their work when they did not have the necessary skill or knowledge. Interviewees were also asked about any barriers to their learning, recurring problems they encountered in their work, and individuals they admired for their learning practice.

Paradoxes and Double Binds

Watkins and Wiswell identified the double binds of staff developers and illustrated them with anecdotes, which they developed both directly from stories told by individuals and from interpretations of stories and incidents pieced together from the accounts of several individuals. These double binds, described here, strongly influenced learning in the organization.

Difficulties in Enacting a Learning Mission. The organization espoused a strong commitment to training and education, but trainers did not seem to understand the role, scope, limits, or time frames of training, nor did they understand the difficulty of balancing the needs of management, staff, educators, and the situations.

Perhaps the best illustration of this problem was offered by a staff developer who said that a manager had recently called to complain about a serious mistake: "I sent Joe to your training session last week as a last resort, and he came back as inefficient as before." Instead of discussing the role and limits of training, the staff developer retorted, "We had him for two days. How long have you had him?"

Another illustration is one respondent's report that she could not keep up with the escalating demand for training. An irate supervisor complained that the education department had asked staff what their inservice needs were, staff had responded, and now they were being put off. Frustrated, the respondent went to her own supervisor and was told to listen attentively to new requests for training, to nod her head so that people would feel heard, and then simply to continue doing as before. This supervisor did not seem aware that such a strategy would simply increase frustration, decrease the credibility of the department, and potentially undermine everyone's belief in the organization's commitment to learning.

Autonomy Versus Equity. Despite an espoused commitment to department autonomy, budget decisions made at the departmental level were often reversed later. The hierarchical chain was also supposed to be followed, but individuals often skipped levels to deal with interpersonal problems and, through the informal chain, "called in I.O.U.'s" to get things done. One respondent reported an incident that illustrated the latter problem. An individual was deemed ill-suited for a particular task by her current acting supervisor, yet both were competing for the same position in the new organizational structure. The person above them both would make the final choice. To the acting supervisor, the only recourse appeared to be discussing this task reassignment with a person two levels above.

Values in Action. One individual commented, "Our budget cuts are setting our direction right now. We don't believe in doing it this way, but what can we do?" A department manager commented that the travel budget had "theoretically" been allocated in an equitable fashion, with each person getting a couple of hundred dollars to go to the conference of his or her choice. In practice, however, additional funds could often be found in special cases. There were no criteria for special cases, nor was this practice public. In another instance, the training staff was given two weeks by top management to develop a chemical safety program for 2,000 employees. This time frame was accepted without challenge, despite the recognition that the resulting program would not be as effective as it could have been.

Which Professional Specialization? Nursing staff developers reported having been asked to drop all their training activity to work in the hospital, and nonnurses were invited to attend "nurse staff developer" meetings. Many nurse educators wanted to maintain their nursing expertise, since they never knew when they would have to go back to nursing. Further, they had often come to staff development because they were outstanding nurses but had little or no training as educators. Prestige in the organization was still tied to nursing proficiency. One person reported that highly skilled practitioners had refused to attend training sessions, since they felt more skilled than the trainers in their specialties. The same respondent then used this situation to justify her emphasis on developing nursing skills instead of staff development skills. Finally, one staff developer said that the person who would be most respected in the field would be a "highly-skilled and up-to-date practitioner who can teach new procedures and who can also explain them to a patient."

Training for Trainers. Many of the respondents had overwhelming teaching commitments, which made it difficult for them to attend any formal staff development activities: "The job comes first; education, second." One person said, "There is no education for the education department." Another said, "Training is for others, not for trainers. You give it to yourself. It's the self-starters who are rewarded." Still another noted that learning was seldom noticed or rewarded unless it led to new program development for the organization. Ironically, the hospital's recently revised continuing education policy said, "The Nursing Department shares responsibility for quality continuing education with those employees whose professional skills require periodic updating." A frequent complaint among these staff developers was that their learners often resisted attending training sessions, saying that they preferred to learn on their own.

Themes for Hospital Staff Development

Reflection on the potential unintended consequences of these tensions, paradoxes, and double binds led to the identification of several themes that clarify the dilemmas of hospital staff development.

In response to the overwhelming demand for programs, staff developers may have focused so hard on educating clients that there appeared to be little time to educate themselves. Over time, if this situation persists, educators may begin to doubt that learning is the organization's mission, since it does not seem available to them, and this perception may in turn affect their long-term competence and satisfaction. If their skill levels deteriorate, they may in fact jeopardize the organization's learning mission. Moreover, if others observe this phenomenon, they may conclude that education is either not very important or that educators think they need less information than others do. On the one hand, this attitude could imply superior knowledge; on the other hand, it could imply that educators do not need to know much to perform their tasks. In all these possibilities, one idea predominates: The lack of inservice activities for educators may well undermine the learning goals of the hospital.

Educators must maintain a high level of professional expertise. There was recurring evidence of high commitment to maintaining professional expertise, but, in this setting, technical expertise was valued over educational expertise. Certainly, the ability to respond quickly to the need for training staff in a new medical procedure is essential; yet, if training is not given in such a way that others learn and become proficient, the outcome will be detrimental for the hospital, and educators may not feel able to maintain their sense of professionalism. By placing a high value on only one aspect of their work, staff developers are less likely to do professional-quality work.

There is a dilemma here: The more a nurse educator seeks to enhance professional expertise, whether in nursing or in continuing education, the more he or she may decrease overall professional expertise. Clark (1979) cites Cooper and Hornback, who suggest that a continuing educator in nursing ought to hold a master's degree in the specialization and a doctorate in adult education. As an alternative, Clark suggests a master's degree in curriculum and instruction. O'Connor (1986) addresses this issue and states that the major role of a continuing nurse educator is that of educator: The individual should be aware of the larger context of continuing professional education of which he or she is a part, should have skill in the design and implementation of learning, and should have subject-matter expertise. Nevertheless, O'Connor also notes that the individual's major professional identity remains that of nurse. She sees the ongoing need for nurse educators to function as role models of competent professional practice.

O'Connor's distinction clarifies the dilemma. One way of viewing either nursing or education is as a calling, a vocation. In this conception, the individual's identity is tied up with fulfilling this role, and a nurse or a teacher is who he or she is—whether at work, unemployed, or at leisure. Furthermore, when a profession is a vocation, the task is open-ended. There is an infinite number of potential "teachable moments," of potential learners, and of potential patients. It is little wonder, then, that nurse educators say, "I'm doing the work of three people" and report that their jobs are overwhelming. O'Connor (1986) gives a more concrete example of the dilemma. A nurse educator is observing trainees who attempt to give patients treatments and do it ineptly. As an educator, she or he must give suggestions and encourage practice; as a nurse, she or he is a patient advocate, who must ensure that no harm is done.

The task of fulfilling both callings at a professional level is staggering, yet one unintended consequence of valuing nursing to the exclusion of giving any training in continuing education is to communicate to the organization that anyone can teach. Ultimately, this message has the greatest potential of undermining the nurse educator's sense of professionalism. Calling in experts, using skilled practitioners to help with subject matter, specializing more narrowly, or moving to more general practice areas are all strategies to augment an individual's technical expertise. Reframing professionalism to include high levels of accountability (if not always personal performance) in both the technical area and the educational area may counter the role overload inherent in this situation.

Equity and autonomy, two values that appear important to many educators, may be intrinsically in conflict. They are in conflict whenever one individual's freedom to act impinges on another's freedom to act. In organizations, this is frequently the case. When travel budgets are prorated equitably to all, for example, individual decision makers feel unable to exercise their authority. If they make exceptions and grant additional funds in special cases, then those whose cases are not special feel that they have not been treated fairly. When interpersonal issues are dealt with outside the normal hierarchy, individuals feel a sense of injustice: "After all, why didn't the person talk to me first?" When budget cuts are made without explicit priority setting, others will conclude that the budget is the implicit priority anyway. By making cuts without critical reflection on the consequences or public discussion of them, the real cost of making those cuts becomes invisible, and staff developers risk having colluded in making further cuts in staff development more likely.

All these actions were taken by this hospital's staff developers. What is particularly poignant is that the developers originally described these actions as having been taken by higher managers and as illustrations of the constraints under which developers worked. Hospital leaders, they said, treated staff development unfairly and did not grant the necessary autonomy to function effectively. That they mirrored this behavior themselves in their own budget cutting and rule bending had not occurred to the developers. A crucial aspect of reflection in action (Schön, 1983) is finding mirrors by which to observe one's own practice. In this instance, the clear observation of the discrepancies between what managers said and did suggests that developers could have served as mirrors to top management. They would also have needed to ask top management to observe their practice. From the perspective of staff development, developers made the final specific cuts in programs, thereby implicitly defining which programs had value, but decried managers for not valuing staff development, since managers had called for the cuts. This displacement of blame for priorities may have the effect of removing educators from responsibility for autonomously defining their own future.

Perhaps it is in hospital staff developers' unawareness of how their practices emulate those they chafe under that they are most likely to convey a hidden curriculum (incidental learning) to their trainees. There is a paradox in a department that seeks to help others observe and correct their mistakes but knows very few ways to get help in observing and correcting itself.

Implications for Hospital-Based Staff Development

These themes suggest that the staff developers in this hospital face complex double binds, with no simple solutions and with potentially harmful consequences for learning. These double binds became visible through an examination of the incidental learning practices of nurse educators and through reflection on the implications of those practices. Nevertheless, staff development, as it is now designed, seldom brings critical reflection on this kind of experience into the classroom, nor is training used to help nurses reflect more on their practice, as Schön (1983) recommends.

A Focus on Action. Tobin, Wise, and Hull (1979) offer a model of the staff development process that includes twenty-three variables depicting the input and planning process, but only three variables for output: implementation, which leads to evaluation and performance. This emphasis on planning over action is typical of the field. Staff development is often only a cluster of workshops and courses that have little relationship to one another. Implementation, in these instances, is different with each iteration. The field knows much more about how to plan for developing staff than about how to help individuals develop a "habit" of continuous learning. Researching one's own practice by videotaping and criticizing one's training, or otherwise experimenting with new behavior followed by reflection, may be one way to begin developing better information on what works and what does not when individual staff actually need development.

Action Learning. Action learning (Pedler, 1983; Revans, 1971) is another approach to making the implementation process more visible. In this model, individuals work in teams on problems similar to their own in other organizations or units. They meet periodically, over a relatively long time, to reflect on whether they have identified the right problem, and they experiment with actions that help them see the problems from different viewpoints. In action learning, implementation is seen as a complex process that includes myriad details, actions, and responses, all of which call for constant interpretations of the meaning of experience. Subjecting actions as well as interpretations to public scrutiny and a careful reexamination of alternative perspectives can help practitioners improve by encouraging them to test their inferences and seek valid data about their practice. Without such reflection, unintended consequences are likely to prevail, and practitioners will be unaware of their contributions to undesired outcomes. Organizational constraints and the intractability of others will be cited as causes for these unintended consequences (Argyris, Putnam, and Smith, 1985).

Revans (1982) reports a study he conducted in 1965 on hospital internal communications. The study illustrates how hospital staff may unconsciously create a culture that represses expressiveness, in turn suppressing learning and problem solving. Observing differential dropout rates among student nurses in five different hospitals, Revans hypothesized that there may have been something about hospital culture that affected dropout rates. He checked to see whether different staff turnover rates also varied by hospital and found that turnover was indeed greater wherever student attrition was greater, as were sickness and absence rates. Moreover, the average patient stays were shorter at the more stable hospitals, and they were longer at less stable hospitals. Measuring staff attitudes, Revans found that hospitals where the ward sisters had confidence in their superiors also treated student nurses sympathetically. He further concluded that if the underlying problem was communication, then socially dependent patients—those with medical rather than surgical needs—would be more affected by hospital differences. This was also confirmed.

To account for these differences, Revans then developed a theory based on a definition of learning as a feedback process, which consists of seeing the effect of one's own behavior. Hospitals are steeped in anxiety and uncertainty. When uncertainty blocks communication, individuals develop unrealistic ideas about themselves (their skills and knowledge, in the case of student nurses; their illness, in the case of patients). Faced with uncertainty, those who do not know the answers discourage further questions. They can then be said to have unrealistically defensive images of their positions. Such defensive images in turn stifle the communication that student nurses need. As a result, they learn little.

How does a hospital break this dysfunctional cycle in order to produce learning? Revans defines action learning as a process that enables learners to develop fresh perceptions of problems and reinterpret past experiences first by working in peer groups to examine problems and then by taking action, with continual group reflection on each new action. For Revans (Pedler, 1983) "responsible action is our greatest disciplinarian as well as our most sympathetic helper" (p. 20). Garratt (1983) and Marsick (1987) depict action learning as action followed by observation of the results of that action, which in turn is followed by reflection, which leads to the development of hypotheses and interpretations about the action and about any future actions that may be needed. At this point, reflection must precede any new action. In this phase, learners experiment with alternative actions, to test their results. This is a group-facilitated cycle of action and reflection. What action learning provides is a process that can interrupt poor communication and insufficient feedback, which are at the heart of the cycle Revans found in the high-turnover hospitals.

Staff developers can use action learning to improve their own delivery skills and to expose paradoxical behavior. Faced with the types of double binds described in the Watkins and Wiswell (1987) study, staff developers must be able to identify the incidental and unintended learning that may result from their actions and to develop approaches that are more consistent with their own espoused values.

Conclusion

This chapter has focused on the incidental learning of staff developers. Just as staff developers may act in ways that lead to results they do not want, so too may their learners be acting inconsistently with espoused values. Critical reflection and dialogue on nursing experiences is a key component of effective nurse education. As Cooper (1983) puts it, formal education is only the tip of the iceberg. To maintain the needed level of professional expertise, staff developers will increasingly rely on self-directed learning and other forms of nonformal and informal learning, for their own development and as a means of fostering development in others.

Textbooks and guidelines from the American Nursing Association provide staff developers with clear and precise information on designing, managing, and teaching various programs. Hospital staff developers are skilled at responding very quickly to urgent training needs with well-developed, structured programs. The case study in this chapter suggests that hospital staff developers must begin to observe carefully what actually happens in the delivery of training and to reflect on the "cultural" impact of trainers' actions—in the classroom and out, in getting training for themselves, in making budget decisions that establish training priorities, and in perpetuating inequities. In short, staff developers must begin by developing themselves.

Hospital staff developers have unique constraints, which may produce double binds that inhibit effectiveness. These double binds tend to produce actions that are inconsistent with values, while keeping people blind to unintended consequences. Only a process of critical reflection, which includes techniques to make individuals' action observable both to themselves and to others, will break the dysfunctional chain. This process is also appropriate for helping others reflect on their own experiences. Routine ways of observing practitioners in action—verbatim accounts, transcripts of audiotapes, videotapes, group observations, role playing—facilitate the process. An essential dimension is a trusted peer group that is willing to disclose and test its inferences. In contrast to prevailing techniques for hospital staff development, this process is less structured and predictable, as well as interpersonally more demanding. Nevertheless, it appears to have the greatest potential for helping practitioners change their behavior and interrupt dysfunctional norms.

References

Argyris, C., Putnam, R., and Smith, D. M. *Action Science: Concepts, Methods, and Skills for Research and Intervention.* San Francisco: Jossey-Bass, 1985.

Argyris, C., and Schön, D. *Organizational Learning: A Theory of Action Perspective.* Reading, Mass.: Addison-Wesley, 1978.

Clark, C. *The Nurse as Continuing Educator.* New York: Springer, 1979.

Cooper, S. *The Practice of Continuing Education in Nursing.* Rockville, Md.: Aspen Systems, 1983.

Del Bueno, D., and Freund, C. *Power and Policies in Nursing Administration: A Casebook.* Owings Mills, Md.: Rynd Communications, 1986.

Garratt, B. "The Power of Action Learning." In M. Pedler (ed.), *Action Learning in Practice.* Aldershot, Hants, England: Gower, 1983.

Levitt, B., and March, J. "Organizational Learning." Unpublished manuscript, 1987.

Marsick, V. "Action Learning at MiL: A Strategy for Empowering Managers." Presentation to the Commission of Professors of Adult Education, Washington, D.C., October 1987.

Moccia, P. "The Nature of the Nursing Shortage: Will Crisis Become Structure?" *Nursing and Health Care,* 1987, *8* (6), 321–322.

Nadler, L. *Designing Training Programs: The Critical Events Model.* Reading, Mass.: Addison-Wesley, 1982.

O'Connor, A. *Nursing Staff Development and Continuing Education.* Boston: Little, Brown, 1986.

Pedler, M. *Action Learning in Practice.* Aldershot, Hants, England: Gower, 1983.

Revans, R. W. *Developing Effective Managers: A New Approach to Business Education.* New York: Praeger, 1971.

Revans, R. W. *The Origins and Growth of Action Learning.* Lund, Sweden: Studentlitteratur, 1982.

Schön, D. *The Reflective Practitioner.* New York: Basic Books, 1983.

Tobin, H., Wise, P., and Hull, P. *The Process of Staff Development: Components for Change.* St. Louis, Mo.: Mosby, 1979.

Watkins, K., and Wiswell, B. "Incidental Learning in the Workplace." Paper presented to the Human Resource Management Organizational Behavior Conference, San Antonio, Texas, 1987.

Karen Watkins is assistant professor of adult education and human resource development at the University of Texas, Austin. She taught for ten years at Miami–Dade Community College, where she also worked in staff, program, and organizational development. She has worked for the National Institute for Staff and Organizational Development.

*Volunteering provides an overlooked but powerful source
of learning that can be instructive to staff developers in all
organizations.*

Tapping the Potential: Learning and Development of Community Volunteers

Boyd E. Rossing

Maintaining vital and productive organizations where the energies and talents of staff can find constructive expression is not a challenge only for corporations or government agencies. It is also a concern of organizations created or served by volunteers. In all these organizations, members must learn and adapt as they encounter new challenges or assume new responsibilities. The demand for such learning is always increasing. This chapter focuses on the special opportunities, challenges, and new directions for learning and development of members of voluntary or volunteer-supported organizations.

Organizational Crisis and the Voluntary Sector

As described in Chapter One, sweeping changes are creating a need to question "business as usual" in today's organizations. Bennis and Nanus (1985) claim that organizations "are experiencing a crisis of governance, the incapacity to cope with the expectations of their constituents . . ." (p. 2). In this time of crisis, the voluntary, nonprofit sector demonstrates some unique approaches to both organizations' and members' learning that may be of use to all organizations.

V. J. Marsick (ed.). *Enhancing Staff Development in Diverse Settings.*
New Directions for Continuing Education, no. 38. San Francisco: Jossey-Bass, Summer 1988.

Volunteer Renaissance. Over the past two decades, America has witnessed a "renaissance of interest in volunteerism" (Langton, 1982). This growing interest has generated an ever-deepening analysis of the meaning of volunteerism and of the nature, scope, and functions of the nonprofit sector. For the purposes of this discussion, two concepts will be treated as partially overlapping: *volunteering* and *the nonprofit sector.* Thus, *volunteering* refers to freely chosen, unpaid individual activity carried out for a variety of motives. Volunteering occurs in all sectors of society but prevails in the nonprofit sector. *The nonprofit sector* refers to nongovernmental activity that serves useful social purposes without competing for profit in the marketplace.

The Voluntary Nonprofit Organization. This sector is extremely diverse, spanning artistic, educational, environmental, health, consumer, civil rights, and religious organizations. Some groups are small and informal; others are large, well financed, and organized through national, state, and local chapters. Many volunteer organizations are attached to and support larger nonprofit or governmental agencies or even commercial firms. Two general purposes characterize voluntary organizations. Some exist exclusively to satisfy the needs or interests of their members. These are called *expressive* organizations. They provide friendship, status, recreation, self-help, spiritual expression, creative outlets, or advancement opportunities for members (Mason, 1985). *Instrumental* organizations pursue broader social goals. In either case, members typically work for personal agendas or ideals, rather than for profit. While the organization may be instrumental, an expressive aspect is also important, particularly in the personal motivations of members. In this way, voluntary organizations often serve as extended families or communities (Mason, 1985).

Volunteer organizations often place more emphasis on pursuing their missions, and less on efficiency of operations. They are typically pluralistic in their goals (Wortman, 1982), while government and for-profit organizations are likely to focus more selectively on parts of the problems. Voluntary organizations also have more open, participatory, nonhierarchical, and nonauthoritative structures and styles of operation. Relationships are close and personal, rather than impersonal. Finally, they tend to operate on a small scale, with closer proximity to their clienteles (Wortman, 1982).

Volunteer Motives and Actions. What about volunteers themselves? How do their motivations differ from those of paid and professional workers? Historically, a sharp distinction has been drawn. Volunteering has been viewed as a self-chosen, intrinsically satisfying activity. Recently, however, the motives for volunteering and for paid employment have become more alike. Workers seek greater opportunities for creativity. Conversely, volunteers and employers alike recognize that volunteer experience can develop job-related skills.

Volunteers and paid workers often approach their tasks differently. The volunteer typically acts on the basis of his or her reservoir of experience and values, without specialized training. A human, responsive, nonprogrammed approach is expected, rather than a trained, professionalized, objective mode. Volunteers "love what they are doing" (White, 1982, p. 154). According to Wortman (1982), volunteers are more likely to approach their missions ideologically, whereas professionals emphasize applying their expertise to goal achievement.

How important is volunteering to the volunteer? Here, as in other areas of volunteerism, we suffer from lack of information. Perhaps it is more important than paid work to the person seeking ideological goals and less important to the person seeking diversion, social contact, or some other nonfinancial benefit. For some individuals, volunteer activity may represent the principal tie to the community. Some volunteers spend many hours every week in their pursuits; others commit only a few hours per year. One survey (Gallup Organization, 1986) indicated that volunteers contribute an average of three and a half hours per week. Clearly, the importance of volunteering varies considerably from one person to another.

The Voluntary Sector's Modeling Function

Langton (1982) argues that the voluntary sector has an increasingly important corrective role to perform as an antidote to the bureaucratic, centralized, and depersonalized features of contemporary government and business. Langton proposes three functions for the "new volunteerism." Through the prophetic function, this sector continually shapes and reshapes the vision of a more just social order. The dramatic growth of citizen advocacy groups reflects this function.

Through the second, supplementary function, the voluntary nonprofit sector provides government-mandated services to supplement government-sector services. Hospitals, for example, receive 40 percent or more of their resources from government.

The third function is modeling. The voluntary sector experiments with new forms of organizational agencies. The modeling function is especially timely today, since a major transformation in thinking about leadership and management is under way in the for-profit sector. Managers are asked to recognize the expressive needs of workers and to appreciate the importance of creativity, organizational values, and long-range vision. Organizations are urged to accept some short-term redundancy and inefficiency by making greater use of participatory structures to enhance human meaning, innovation, and empowerment. More attention is focused on informal, on-the-job development, as a contrast to and a point of integration with formal training.

Many of these developments, new to the private sector, have always been found in the nonprofit sector. Greenberg (1983) notes that business now advocates such concepts as collaborative team management, networking, flattening the hierarchical pyramid, and valuing the contributions of workers. Many of these have guided volunteer management for years. By and large, however, little mention of voluntary, nonprofit exemplars is found in the literature on corporate transformation. Nevertheless, the concepts underlying the transformation in corporate leadership are not applied systematically in the literature to the voluntary sector, either. Perhaps these ideas are still too new and too oriented toward business. What is more likely is that few people have studied how to apply these concepts to the nonprofit sector.

Volunteer Learning, Training, and Development: Practice and Literature

Formal and Informal Training. Leaders in the volunteer field have long advocated high-quality training and development of volunteers (Naylor, 1976; Stenzel and Feeney, 1976), but the nature and amount of formal training provided for volunteers has not been documented. According to Wortman (1982), managers in volunteer organizations rarely receive any type of formal training or development, and middle managers and top executives receive the least of all. Little developmental programming is conducted for volunteer staff, either. Volunteer organizations "assume that the staff is developing itself" (p. 179). Sophisticated training programs are most likely to be developed at the national level by large volunteer organizations. Smaller, local volunteer groups often give low priority to training, because few resources are available to support it. Organizational leaders do not know enough about volunteer training to lobby for it. They usually have many other concerns on their minds, since they often perform multiple roles.

Part of the reason why volunteer training and development practices vary so much is that needs for volunteer development differ. Many volunteers take on responsibilities in organizations where they already have sufficient knowledge and skills to carry them out; their primary motivation is to use their knowledge and skills to provide service. In these cases, it may be insulting to imply that volunteers need development or education. At the other extreme, some volunteers land in situations where they are quite unprepared; they jump in because something truly needs doing, and they care enough to try.

The Training-Learning Process. A fairly common pattern of recommendations can be found in the literature on volunteer training. Most writers advocate a continuous training-learning process that yields an orderly progression in knowledge, skill, understanding, and experience

(Stenzel and Feeney, 1976; Byron, 1974; O'Connell, 1976). The process is typically described in several steps. The first one is recruitment, which can be used to provide information and orient the prospective volunteer to the organization. Next comes the placement interview, which Byron (1974) sees as a learning process. Formats for orientation and preservice, the third step, vary by organization and requirements; more preservice training is needed when volunteers provide direct services to clients. Sometimes this need is met by provision of a kind of apprenticeship to seasoned staff. The literature recommends that this training be continued on the job and supported by learning gained through staff meetings, practical assignments, and special readings. Inservice training should then be provided periodically through refresher courses, special-occasion meetings, advanced training, interorganizational activities, and team building. Newsletters, performance evaluation, and volunteer-recognition activities (Byron, 1974) can also support learning. Finally, some organizations have adopted self-development plans (Stenzel and Feeney, 1976). While all these practices are commonly advocated, it is clear that they are better suited to some volunteer settings than to others and that many volunteer organizations are not able to follow this advice.

Volunteer Development Responsibilities. Responsibility for helping volunteers learn also varies widely in different volunteer settings. Sometimes volunteer development is equated with formal orientation and training. Either organizations employ volunteer coordinators, with responsibility for arranging orientation, or staff share this responsibility (O'Connell, 1976). Sometimes volunteers learn informally, and no one has either training or even coordinating responsibility. In these cases, volunteer development may be equated with learning from experience. In organizations where professionals and volunteers work together, learning and development are increasingly viewed as a partnership responsibility (Implications of Volunteerism in Extension Study, 1987).

Under these varied circumstances, what kinds of volunteer learning and development actually occur, particularly in organizations where the training function is minimal? The volunteer field, with fewer resources than organizations have in the government and for-profit sectors, has necessarily relied to a great extent on informal "learning by doing" as a source of members' development (and, of course, informal learning is part of the concept of volunteering). What does research tell us about volunteers' learning and development, particularly through informal opportunities?

New Insights from Research on Volunteers' Learning

Learning in Different Contexts. One recent study explores the meaning of volunteering to volunteers' sense of mission and citizenship and the importance of various modes of learning experienced by volunteers (Fiset and others, 1987). The results suggest that "volunteering is perceived as an important form of self-development . . . volunteering in general is a powerful learning context for individuals, and . . . learning, as a motive for volunteers, is not static, but rather evolves" (p. 75). Four kinds of volunteer organizations were studied: *institutionally directed* (a national literacy volunteer organization or a corporate volunteer agency), *volunteer group–directed* (a semiautonomous guild in a hospital, a museum, or a public television station), *problem-directed* (a volunteer fire department, a hospital, or an education board), and *social change–directed* (the women's movement, the peace movement). In this study, the context greatly influenced types of learning opportunities. For example, a literacy volunteer received explicit training in literacy skills, but an association volunteer was expected to learn by doing. The authors offer a tentative framework for comparing the types of learning found among volunteers in different contexts. Their discussion is preliminary, but it does afford insight into the complex relationships between volunteering and learning. The authors suggest that institution-directed settings promote instrumental and didactic learning, and that social and expressive learning prevails in volunteer group-directed settings. Problem-directed organizations place a premium on learning for problem solving. Finally, learning in social change-directed organizations occurs principally in the critical-reflexive mode.

Learning in Community Groups. Two other studies—Whitmore and others (1986) and Rossing (1987a)—have focused more specifically on learning from and through the experience of participating in voluntary, community-based organizations. Whitmore and others (1986) interviewed volunteers in rural, locally originated community groups. The groups' concerns ranged from social action (civil rights, the environment, peace) to problem solving (housing, energy) to leisure services (for senior citizens, for youth, for a historical society). The study focused on informal learning through group participation. Three significant dimensions were identified: learning about internal group dynamics versus external factors affecting group action, gaining knowledge versus skill, and learning about oneself versus learning about others. Learning across these categories was broadest for those in groups seeking changes in the larger social or political environment. Persons with the most experience had the most difficulty identifying what they were learning from their current involvements versus what had come from the past. The study also highlighted group conditions that facilitate or retard participation and learning. A social climate of acceptance was critical. Information from outside the group was accepted best when group participants had control over the flow of such information. Finally, members of groups with limited goals were more satisfied and gained greater confidence from these group experiences than members did who were striving for complex goals.

The Learning-by-Doing Process. Rossing (1987a) investigated the learning of group skills by thirty-seven members of voluntary, community problem-solving groups. Members were interviewed and described their beliefs regarding effective group functioning. They also discussed previous experiences that had contributed to the development of their beliefs. Beliefs fell into four categories: those relevant to the group leader, to group members, to the group as a whole, and to the broader spectrum of human behavior and community problem solving. One question at the heart of the study was "Do learners, appropriately or inappropriately, transfer beliefs acquired in one setting to practice in another, potentially different, setting?" Most often, interviewees generalized their beliefs to all group situations. Only in rare instances did they tailor a belief to a particular situation (for example, prescribing a loose structure for a short-term project and a tight one for a long-term project).

The Rossing (1987a) study sheds further light on the learning-by-doing process. Participants themselves frequently emphasized that involvement in community groups is a learning experience, but many were not immediately conscious of their learning and had difficulty articulating what they had learned. They said, "You get involved and you learn, and you know you have learned, but it is difficult to state specifically what you learned and how it occurred." For example, a third of the interviewees could not recall any event that had prompted a change in their beliefs. Most were able to recall some learning instances. The events that were recalled were often characterized by vivid emotional content: frustration or pain, surprise or challenge, or gratifying success. In most cases, people had revised their beliefs in response to obstacles that contradicted their expectations.

In terms of the timing of learning events, Rossing's findings were similar to those of Whitmore and others (1986). Most learning occurred sometime after the volunteer's initial entry into community activities. Few volunteers, especially those with considerable group experience, reported learning from very recent or current experiences. Finally, group leaders typically reported learning about their leadership roles. Surprisingly, almost no group leaders recalled learning new things about members' behavior. Members reported a broader range of learning than leaders did. Members did report learning about members' behavior, as well as about groups' and leaders' behavior.

Patterns of Volunteer Learning. All the studies of volunteer learning mentioned so far are exploratory. They were based on small samples and concentrated on in-depth individual interviews. Their results do not conclusively demonstrate the nature and amount of learning that occurs in volunteer settings, but they do present an outline of likely patterns. Together, they suggest the following conclusions:

- Volunteering is a powerful source of learning
- Volunteers value that learning

- Formal training of volunteers varies according to context
- Volunteers acquire a broad range of knowledge and skills
- The nature of learning varies according to group context and role of the volunteer
- Learning by doing varies according to group conditions
- Volunteers have difficulty articulating their learning
- Volunteers tend to overgeneralize the benefits they have formed from their experiences
- As volunteers accumulate experience in similar situations, their new learning from such experience declines.

New Directions for Volunteers' Learning and Development

Integration of Classroom and On-the-Job Learning. Classroom and on-the-job learning differ in some important ways. Coleman (1976) suggests that classroom learning is largely symbolic, while on-the-job learning is experiential. Each form of learning has strengths and weaknesses. The strengths of experiential, informal learning are intrinsic motivation, direct link to further actions, and retention. The strengths of symbolic, formal learning are efficiency and transmission of past knowledge. The weaknesses of experiential learning are difficulty in extracting principles from experience and the amount of time required. Symbolic learning suffers from dependence on language, the difficulty of applying theory to action, and the need to create motivation in the learner.

Volunteers' development will be strengthened in the future by a greater appreciation of the complementary features of both types of learning. Current literature in the field tends to focus primarily on classroom learning, whereas practice emphasizes informal learning. A body of research on informal learning and its relationship to formal training is being created; the challenge is to build and apply a similar but context-relevant body of knowledge to the volunteer sector. One example of such research is an evaluation study of volunteer leaders (Rossing, 1987b). The study found that the planning and directing skills are most likely to be strengthened by training, but that attitudes change more because of informal learning through experience.

Strengthening Learning from Experience. An important new direction for volunteer development concerns understanding and expanding the capacity of individuals to profit from their experiences. To quote Cell (1984), "Our experiential learning is often dysfunctional, always incomplete. We need to use present experience to test our beliefs, correcting the misinterpretations we've made, lifting the veils we've placed between ourselves and reality" (p. 177).

Studies of volunteers' learning show that many individuals have considerable difficulty articulating their beliefs about why their activities are successful. Schön (1983) suggests that "reflection in action," or behavior without conscious reflection, is adequate for routine activities, but it is insufficient when new problems arise. Under those circumstances, the ability to reflect on one's belief is crucial to the development of new, adaptive solutions.

To further enhance the likelihood of volunteers' learning through experience, formal preparatory and supplementary educational opportunities can be provided. Such programs might strengthen observation, thinking, communication, creativity, and evaluation and can directly assist experiential learning, as well as provide concepts that volunteers can directly test and apply in later experiences. Another method of enhancing such learning is to have individuals pursue more consciously what their learning situations offer. A journal is a valuable tool to consider. According to Cell (1984), journals increase the intensity and depth of experiential learning.

Selecting Learning Opportunities. The studies already reviewed in this chapter indicate that different kinds of learning are available across different settings, different roles, and different tasks within settings. These findings can be used to plan for progressively higher performance in citizen and volunteer development. A volunteer assignment should provide a challenge, contain some novelty, and offer the kinds of learning the volunteer is ready to obtain. Coordinators, veteran members, and other facilitators can help ensure that the volunteer has enough time in any situation to gain the learning he or she seeks. Finally, veteran members can help the new volunteer to anticipate and take advantage of the learning potential of surprising, challenging, or promising situations, as well as of difficulties and setbacks.

Organizational Conditions. The research on volunteers' learning provides some indication of the conditions that favor learning from experience. A sense of belonging, opportunities to contribute to group effort, and sharing of concerns, ideas, and feelings—all these factors contribute to satisfaction and to learning from experience. In the future, volunteers will pay more attention to the role of organizational conditions in shaping and supporting learning and to establishing and changing the norms that support organizational goals and learning.

Volunteering as a System of Learning Relationships. Today's organizations are experiencing a crisis of expectations and change. Staff can learn from one another as they experiment with new ways of working together. Volunteers also learn across organizational settings as they exchange insights with coworkers, covolunteers and family members. McCauley (1986) suggests that relationships with others can help individuals acquire information, learn roles, and obtain feedback on their own strengths and weaknesses. Volunteers frequently report gaining new insights by discussing their experiences with their spouses and community leaders. This kind of exchange can be a tremendous aid to learning. Learning relationships can be formally established through mentoring, coaching, or sponsoring programs or through the establishment of support groups. Such relationships can also be encouraged and supported informally.

The challenge is to create a continual process of education, whereby insights derived from practical experience are distilled and communicated to others. Work on tools to aid in distilling the lessons of experience is now under way (Boud, Keogh, and Walker, 1985). Such tools promise to turn organizations and communities into learning laboratories.

Support for Volunteer Learning and Development. To meet the increased developmental needs of volunteers, especially in small organizations, new means of generating or tapping educational resources must be employed. Ray (1982) advocates the use of networks of volunteer organizations that pool resources. He cites a statewide effort in Colorado that linked the Office of Voluntary Citizen Participation with United Way to enhance promotion, referral, and training. Ray also suggests that organizations exploit the resources of higher education. Through partnerships with volunteer centers and organizations, universities and colleges can provide training, assist in program evaluation, and conduct needed research on effective volunteer participation. Support can also be expected from those concerned with revitalizing for-profit organizations, as they come to appreciate the modeling function of the volunteer sector.

Conclusion

A great deal more learning goes on in volunteer organizations than is generally appreciated or understood. This learning is an enormously underused social resource. Opportunities for recognizing and deepening such learning are being missed, and a rich source of insights into organizational effectiveness is being overlooked. Perhaps the most important new direction is simply to document and thereby publicize the significant untapped learning potential of the volunteering impulse.

References

Bennis, W., and Nanus, B. *Leaders: Strategies for Taking Charge.* New York: Harper & Row, 1985.

Boud, D., Keogh, R., and Walker, D. *Reflection: Turning Experience into Learning.* New York: Nichols, 1985.

Byron, E. "Recruiting and Training of Volunteers." In J. Cull and R. Hardy (eds.), *Volunteerism: An Emerging Profession.* Springfield, Ill.: Thomas, 1974.

Cell, E. *Learning to Learn from Experience.* Albany: State University of New York Press, 1984.

Coleman, J. C. "Differences Between Experiential and Classroom Learning." In M. T. Keeton and Associates (eds.), *Experiential Learning: Rationale, Characteristics, and Assessment.* San Francisco: Jossey-Bass, 1976.

Fiset, J., Freeman, D., Ilsley, P., and Snow, B. "Adult Learning in Volunteer Settings: A Neglected Connection." Paper presented to the Adult Education Research Conference, Laramie, Wyoming, May 1987.

Gallup Organization. *Americans Volunteer, 1985.* Report conducted for the Independent Sector. Princeton, N.J.: Gallup Organization, 1986.

Greenberg, E. "Volunteerism—In Spite of the Questions, We Persist." *Mount Holyoke Alumnae Quarterly,* 1983, *67* (2).

Implications of Volunteerism in Extension Study. *Recommendations for Enhancing Extension-Volunteer Programs.* Madison: University of Wisconsin–Madison, 1987.

Langton, S. "The New Volunteerism." In J. Harmon (ed.), *Volunteerism in the Eighties.* Washington, D.C.: University Press of America, 1982.

McCauley, C. D. *Developmental Experiences in Managerial Work: A Literature Review.* Greensboro, N.C.: Center for Creative Leadership, 1986.

Mason, D. "Dealing with Antimanagement Bias in the Third Sector." Paper presented to the annual meeting of the Association of Voluntary Action Scholars, New Orleans, October 1985.

Naylor, H. *Leadership for Volunteering.* New York: Dryden Associates, 1976.

O'Connell, B. *Effective Leadership in Voluntary Organizations.* New York: Association Press, 1976.

Ray, G. "Meeting Volunteers on Their Own Ground." In E. M. Greenberg (ed.), *New Partnerships: Higher Education and the Nonprofit Sector.* New Directions for Experiential Learning, no. 18. San Francisco: Jossey-Bass, 1982.

Rossing, B. "Enhancing Citizen Participation Capacity—The Learning Value of Action Experiences." Paper presented to the annual meeting of the Association of Voluntary Action Scholars, Kansas City, 1987a.

Rossing, B. *Report of the Wisconsin C.E.S. Leadership Impact Study.* Madison: University of Wisconsin Extension, 1987b.

Schön, D. *The Reflective Practitioner.* New York: Basic Books, 1983.

Stenzel, A., and Feeney, H. *Volunteer Training and Development: A Manual.* New York: Seabury Press, 1976.

White, O. "Professionalization of Volunteer Organizations as a 'Problem' in the Theory of Human Action." In J. Harmon (ed.), *Volunteerism in the Eighties.* Washington, D.C.: University Press of America, 1982.

Whitmore, E., Sappington, H., Compton, J., and Greene, J. *Adult Learning Through Participation in Rural Community Groups.* Ithaca, N.Y.: Hatch Research Project, Cornell University, 1986.

Wortman, M. "A Radical Shift from Bureaucracy to Strategic Management in Voluntary Organizations." In J. Harmon (ed.), *Volunteerism in the Eighties.* Washington, D.C.: University Press of America, 1982.

Boyd E. Rossing is assistant professor of continuing education and extension leadership specialist at the University of Wisconsin–Madison. He studies community leadership and provides leadership education for extension staff and community leaders.

*The emergence of a guiding framework for faculty
development in the community college is nowhere more
evident than at Miami–Dade and Los Medanos.*

Community College Faculty Development: Designing a Learning Organization

Sandra C. Acebo, Karen Watkins

Faculty development in the community college has evolved from a collection of ad hoc activities to a professional function. The National Council for Staff, Program, and Organizational Development enables members to maintain contact, holds conferences, and sponsors studies. The National Institute for Staff and Organizational Development sponsors a conference for master teachers and disseminates effective teaching practices through its publications, *Linkages* and *Innovation Abstracts*, on the assumption that teaching excellence is the mission of faculty development. Yet community college faculty development practices have lacked a strong theoretical grounding. It is difficult to showcase exemplary practices or even to identify them without a guiding framework.

This chapter traces efforts toward establishing a guiding framework for community college faculty development. It emphasizes a shift in focus, away from individual faculty growth and toward organizational learning. We shall show how assessment has highlighted the need for excellence in teaching and learning, how teacher-initiated classroom feedback serves this purpose, and how community colleges illustrate initiatives in these directions. The last two sections of this chapter describe

V. J. Marsick (ed.). *Enhancing Staff Development in Diverse Settings.*
New Directions for Continuing Education, no. 38. San Francisco: Jossey-Bass, Summer 1988.

two model programs, at Miami–Dade and Los Medanos, that illustrate aspects of this emerging framework.

Toward a Guiding Framework for Community College Faculty Development

Over the years, a number of authors have sought to develop a guiding framework for faculty development at the community college. Described by some as the mother of community college staff development, Zion (1979) wrote that the idea of a program philosophically oriented toward organizational development has gained momentum. The idea has currency because "a development effort cannot be piecemeal. Curricular innovations cannot be separated from the staff's development as human beings, nor can classroom innovation be separated from the total organizational innovation" (p. 28). Further, any changes in one part of a system affect all other parts. Finally, the program itself must be adaptive to model the "growth, change, and responsiveness that it is asking others to demonstrate by reassessing goals, strategies, and offerings every year" (p. 28). Zion's vision exceeded current practice, which had been largely focused on small-scale projects and inservice workshops, yet her focus on the organization, and not just on the individual, recurs as faculty developers seek a guiding framework or paradigm.

Cooper (1984) studied five programs in the Midwest to validate a comprehensive paradigm for staff, program, and organizational development in the community college. He began with a definition: "planned activities within the community college which are designed to have the potential for improving individual performance, program effectiveness, or the organizational environment and its achievement of goals" (p. 7). Cooper's paradigm thus covered personal, program, and organizational development, each of which was divided into seven processes: purposes, planning, organization and staffing, funding, programming, rewards and incentives, and evaluation. Cooper did not find all twenty-one elements in all community colleges but hypothesized that the absence of any component weakened the overall program. He found that identified leadership was key to staff development: "Staff development which is everyone's responsibility is no one's responsibility" (p. 19).

Nevertheless, there are barriers that make it, paradoxically, both necessary and difficult to implement a comprehensive program. Richardson (1979) observed that community colleges attempt to develop a high level of commitment in order to have maximum access to their human resources, while faculty and staff attempt to limit their contributions to what they perceive to be a fair exchange. Hence, faculty development is designed to get faculty to increase their personal sense of what they can fairly contribute. Under these conditions, faculty development will be effective when it helps people do those things they already want to do or offers rewards or incentives to encourage faculty to do more. Further, an organization must impose sanctions on those not contributing their fair share, but this may extinguish loyalty and commitment. Faculty development may also emphasize information, rather than values, which makes it a less viable vehicle for developing new priorities or for institutional renewal (p. 5). Involving participants in identifying the problems faculty development is intended to solve may help to increase its potential.

Richardson's view of an institutionalized, tacit quid pro quo is similar to Lippitt's (1980) perception that an individual's personal development profoundly affects his or her professional development and the quality of work life. Professional development programs should support individualized action plans that achieve this balance between personal and professional needs.

Faculty must also perceive the need for any development activities that are offered. Chait and Gueths (1981) quote a study by Blackburn, in which 90 percent of the faculty surveyed at twenty-four colleges and universities viewed themselves as above-average or superior teachers. They then suggest criteria for the design of programs that will meet the needs of those who already see themselves as proficient. Their criteria focus more on professional roles and activities associated with faculty status than on organizational needs with a developmental (versus a remedial) approach. They note research by Siegel and Blackburn, who say that helping faculty think about *what* to teach, require, and emphasize is more likely to improve faculty effectiveness than showing them *how* to teach.

A New Guiding Framework

The concept of organizational learning addresses the preceding issues and helps define a guiding framework for faculty development. Organizational learning is defined as the process that enables an organization to change in response to new demands from its environment, just as individual learning occurs when one acquires new resources in the form of skills, knowledge, or values that better equip one to manage one's world. Community colleges need a learning system that enables them to better observe themselves and to use their slack learning resources to adapt. To observe themselves, they need pertinent and timely data on student outcomes by program, course, and degree. They also need data on student and faculty skills. In short, they need accurate information on how they are doing now in order to launch development efforts in a targeted fashion that will lead them to where they want to go.

Slack resources are those that are not being used or are only partly used. They can be anything from money to talents and skills among faculty. A long-term view of faculty development, which is part of the process of developing an organizational learning framework, would encourage community colleges to continuously upgrade the skills and abilities of their faculty, since this is their most critical slack learning resource—and, happily, the most effective for dealing with the programmatic changes community colleges routinely must make. Without slack resources, organizations cannot offer new programs or services or adapt to environmental changes, such as new legislation.

Benveniste (1987) discusses other conditions for organizational learning. Organizational learning requires multiple efforts at addressing complex issues and autonomy for professionals to give them room to act. Finally, staff must see themselves as professionals, participate in national professional reference groups, share commitment to an enobling mission, and talk openly about ethical issues.

Such an approach to faculty development emphasizes an informal learning system, in which faculty are encouraged to participate in their professional networks and to seek self-directed learning that enables them to accomplish new tasks. In relying on a sense of professionalism, this strategy also places a major responsibility on the organization to openly share data regarding discrepancies between current and desired results and to encourage faculty discussion of the ethical implications of current practice. Only by doing this will faculty have the information they need to engage in meaningful problem solving.

Some Examples

Several community colleges do help faculty develop a personal and organizational learning system. Humber College in Toronto, Ontario, uses learning-contract projects of up to two month's duration (Saxton, 1985). Projects have included working in a British Airways tariffs department for one week, to learn procedures and fare structures, and taking a course at another college to learn the skills of horseshoeing.

Yukon College has provided a one-year program of senior undergraduate work in adult education, taught by instructors from the University of British Columbia's Department of Adult Education (Senkpiel, 1986). Through it, faculty have developed a community in which they can "objectively examine their philosophies, their profession, their students and institution" (p. 2). In this model, learning is flexible and relevant, and faculty are able to raise tough issues regarding the ethical bases of their practice.

The programs at Humber and Yukon illustrate ways to develop the skills of individual faculty. The programs at Miami–Dade Community College and Los Medanos College, still to be described, illustrate large-scale, organizationwide approaches to developing an organizational learning system.

Assessment as a Faculty Development Tool

At last count, eleven state legislatures had mandated outcomes-assessment measures for public postsecondary institutions (Halpern, 1987, p. 1). Most often, states have made individual institutions responsible for developing local assessment plans (Boyer and others, 1987, p. 11). Outcomes assessment is designed to certify that a graduate of a community college or a university has college-level competence in basic skills.

The nudge toward accountability is felt most keenly at community colleges. The community college is by nature a talent incubator for the dispossessed and uncertain, as well as an academic alternative for traditional students. These institutions must simultaneously maintain open access and high expectations for students who are often unprepared, psychologically or educationally, for college study. Interviews show that seventy-six community college faculty who taught in twenty different colleges (Seidman, 1987) reached the same conclusion: Despite high standards for college work, it was becoming impossible to uphold them; large-scale entrance and exit assessments had made dramatically visible what faculty may have only suspected before. In fact, a large majority of students now lack the basic skills for courses. Fewer and fewer community college students are transferring to upper-level colleges and universities. Community college faculty are finding that they must now begin to teach students at a point far below where they used to begin.

In this context, professional development ceases to be a luxury and becomes an institutional imperative. Very, very few community colleges can rely any longer on admitting already well-prepared and well-motivated students who guarantee the success of their programs. Instead, faculty must be prepared to deal with academically disadvantaged students and more motivated than ever before to take on this enormous task. Piecemeal development programs, which offer scattered workshops on microcomputers or retirement plans, sabbatical projects, and rewards for improving subject-matter expertise, barely begin to address the need. Even less helpful is the practice of one mandatory inservice day per semester, with a "visiting fireperson" talking about the latest fad. Colleges have begun to recognize that the key to better learning is better teaching, and they key to better teaching is better information about one's results in terms of student learning, student progress, and student responses to one's instructional efforts. The move toward assessment has thus highlighted the needs of community college students, leading to large-scale development programs aimed at teaching faculty skills for which their discipline-based educations never trained them.

Traditionally, faculty are well prepared in their subject matter but less so in teaching and learning strategies. They usually learn through trial and error as teachers and through their own experience as students.

Community colleges stress a teaching mission, require significantly more classroom contact hours from their faculty, and place considerably less emphasis on research and publication than universities do. Knowledge of the learning process is thus at least as important as knowledge of the subject area. In recent years, research has begun to focus on cognitive development, learning styles, cultural differences, and the effectiveness of a variety of new teaching strategies. The key is to make these findings available while faculty are engaged in a continuing and intellectually stimulating examination of their work. Disseminating these findings was the original aim of *Innovation Abstracts.* More recently, the publication has focused on having practitioners describe what works for them. Both objectives give community college faculty information they can use to improve their teaching.

Cross (1987b) was among the first to characterize the new student and the first to recognize that a revolution must take place from "teaching as telling" to "teaching for learning." She advocates that teachers become involved in research on their practice, to provide themselves with formative feedback that will further this revolution. The twin advantages of classroom research are "developing more competent, knowledgeable, classroom teachers who are intellectually challenged by the study of teaching and learning in the discipline, while also adding to our cumulative knowledge of teaching and learning." (p. 9). Many institutions, such as Brookdale Community College, the Community College of Philadelphia, and Sacramento City College, encourage classroom research projects by individual staff members.

Two programs that involve large faculty groups in classroom research, for both professional and institutional development, are the Teaching/Learning Project at Miami–Dade Community College and the Student Development Assessment Project at Los Medanos College. These are taking shape quite differently, as befits the colleges' unique settings and histories, but both programs are based on confidence in the professional judgment of teachers, on a belief in teaching for learning, on the faith that the best faculty development occurs when faculty develop new skills and test them in their own classrooms, and on the assumption that excellence is measured by the benefits accruing to students.

Miami–Dade's Teaching/Learning Project

Miami–Dade is engaged in a major effort to identify characteristics of faculty excellence and to tie that information to hiring, tenure, and promotion policies that reward good teachers. Miami–Dade has launched a multiyear, institutionwide project to improve the quality of teaching and learning, make teaching a professionally rewarding career, and make teaching and learning the focal points of college activities and decision-making processes.

Two graduate-level courses will be required of new faculty at Miami–Dade who are applying for tenure and of experienced faculty who are seeking promotion. One course will deal with teaching and learning in the community college, particularly with reference to the ethnic and cultural diversity of Miami–Dade students. The sequel will prepare faculty to perform their own classroom research. At tenure or promotion time, faculty will be expected to present portfolios documenting their efforts to employ effective teaching methods and assessments of results. This will involve a sizable group of new tenurable faculty, since nearly a third of the college's nine hundred full-time faculty are expected to retire in the next five to seven years.

As is the norm at Miami–Dade, faculty themselves are taking an active role in these reforms. Subcommittees, with broad representation from all four campuses and from a variety of disciplines and cultural backgrounds, are defining the characteristics of faculty excellence, recommending employment and orientation procedures, improving the quality of support from nonteaching units of the college, and planning the prospective courses.

A subcommittee on institutional values laid the foundation for this project with a report completed in 1987 and representing a remarkable level of agreement for such a large organization. The final document places a high value on learning, change, access with quality, diversity, respect for individuals, systematic decision making, and the college's relationship with its service community.

The Faculty Excellence Subcommittee reported a similar collegewide concern for learning, on the basis of a survey of faculty, students, and administrators. Questioned about the characteristics of good teachers, respondents gave "knowledgeable about their work" the highest rating, but five of the top seven items were in the interpersonal area, including treating students with respect, presenting ideas clearly, being enthusiastic, evaluating fairly, listening attentively, and responding to student needs.

Classroom Research. Faculty from across the institution were invited to take part in two-week pilot workshops and to prepare themselves for research on their practice. The workshops provided twenty-two participating teachers with the following four skills, needed to effectively assess learning in their classrooms:

1. Defining and ranking their own specific teaching goals for particular classes
2. Identifying the most useful and appropriate outcomes for assessing attainment of teaching goals
3. Developing, adapting, and refining simple and effective techniques from a prepared handbook
4. Designing management pilot projects to try out selected assessment techniques.

One simple assessment strategy is the "minute paper" (Wilson, 1986). At the end of the class period, the instructor asks students to take a minute and write the answers to two questions: "What is the most important thing you learned today? What questions remain uppermost in your mind as we conclude this class session?" Instructors have been startled by the results. According to Cross (1987a, p. 14), teachers have used minute papers to prepare handouts explaining particularly difficult concepts or to plan review sessions for upcoming class periods.

Future Expectations. Miami–Dade will establish faculty chairs as part of a system to reward excellent teachers. This is a common form of recognition in universities, where exceptional scholars are funded by special endowments. Miami–Dade believes that its own exceptional teachers are equally worthy of such recognition. A $75,000 endowment has been raised for each of nine teaching chairs, with a goal of funding one hundred. Each chair holder will receive special compensation in the form of a large supplemental annual salary grant, plus additional money to be used at the individual's discretion for professional travel, books, materials, clerical assistance, or other work-related activities. The teaching chairs are one more element of a comprehensive program to put teaching excellence at the center of professional development at Miami–Dade.

Los Medanos College's Student Development Assessment Project

Los Medanos College, on the eastern edge of the San Francisco Bay area, by all outward appearances could not differ more from Miami–Dade. It sits between two small river towns in what used to be an industrial hub but is quickly becoming a suburb of San Francisco. With some seventy full-time faculty, it is less than one-tenth the size of Miami–Dade. Planning sessions, with all faculty meeting in one room, are a regular occurrence.

What these two colleges have in common is a history of institutional initiatives to improve student learning. Indeed, the projects reported here have spanned almost a decade for both institutions. Since its opening in 1973, Los Medanos has continued to refine a general education plan unique in its systematic and sequential emphasis on critical thinking and ethical development as key outcomes for the associate degree. Rather than starting with the student intake and monitoring systems for which Miami–Dade is famous, Los Medanos started with a careful definition of the competencies that college graduates should be expected to have and made a conscious decision to structure its program for rehearsal of these competencies throughout the twenty-six units of general education. This brought Los Medanos its own national acclaim. Now, like Miami–Dade, Los Medanos is turning to assessment as a way for faculty to get better insight into student learning. Key elements of the program are planned by an interdisciplinary team with mutually agreed-upon goals, and assessment at Los Medanos is also using a team approach.

Learning Goals at Los Medanos. Learning goals are quite deliberately higher-order outcomes. High value is placed on serving the public good, as well as the individual needs of students. Beyond literate, knowledgeable, and employable graduates, the college seeks to develop students with a perspective larger than their own community and their own lives. Graduates are expected to approach social problems with an analytical skill that is tolerant of ambiguity and divergent viewpoints. Learning goals include the ability to define a social issue, identify competing solutions for issues ranging from personal to national and international problems, evaluate solutions according to ethical considerations, and to choose and support a solution.

Learning experiences sequentially introduce and reinforce higher levels of affective and cognitive development across the curriculum. To broaden perspectives, all six introductory general education courses teach content by using examples that stress global concerns, pluralism, and the ethical implications of knowledge. Two sequel courses lead students through a process of ethical analysis. These interdisciplinary courses, one general and one specific, bring insight from several fields to bear on such current social problems as racism, nuclear proliferation, and the deterioration of the family.

Measuring Adult Education. Now that this plan has been in place for several years, the faculty who inspired it are becoming curious about its effects on students. Are students really becoming more open-minded and capable of empathy? Are their reasoning structures more complex? Older students seem to make greater gains than recent high school graduates do. Can this observation be verified? If so, what causes these differences? On a more practical level, how can the college document the success of its nontraditional program to a traditional university system, which views its demanding interdisciplinary offerings as insufficiently rigorous?

Looking for answers to these questions, the faculty and the dean have progressed through their own assessment-centered faculty development project to a much more sophisticated understanding of student development. Instruments based on the work of development psychologists, such as those intended to measure moral reasoning development (Kohlberg, 1976) and intellectual and ethical development (Perry, 1968), assist faculty both in program evaluation and in learning more about their own and students' patterns of thinking and maturing intellectually. These cognitive models assume that there are sequential, hierarchical stages or levels of development that represent qualitative differences in the ways different individuals approach the same task or issue.

One benefit of looking at tests, to measure students' placement at Perry's and Kohlberg's stages, has been a sense of appreciation for and kinship with the four-year schools doing research on cognitive development. Notably, Kitchener and King's finding (Bowen, 1987) that "reflective judgment" does not generally arrive until the middle or late twenties helps faculty understand why older students often handle controversy better. Also of value is the work of Knefelkamp, Widick, and Parker (1978), who devised a method of developmental instruction based on the Perry scheme and adjusted for diversity, learning activity, degree of structuring of assignments, and level of person encouragement. Their methods succeeded in furthering students' movement from dualism to relativistic thinking, a change many college students never accomplish.

The simple notion that dualistic thinkers (which includes most beginning college students) need a great deal of structure and support, whereas relativistic thinkers need more challenge and responsibility, is very helpful to faculty. Even more important is the underlying developmental assumption that all people have the potential to grow intellectually and ethically, and that teachers can enhance this natural process and observe it in themselves.

Faculty Working Together. Having looked at the literature and taken the tests themselves, a team of faculty working with their dean conducted cross-sectional assessments in 1987 to measure student growth in the three levels of general education courses, from distribution requirements through the social-issues courses. Pre- and posttests on both instruments were given to three course sections at each of the three levels. Analysis of the results should help faculty answer some of their questions about correlations between ethnicity and stage development and the relationship between literacy and stage development or between faculty members' developmental stages and those of students.

The more questions that are answered, the more will arise. One of the most penetrating is whether the developmental models discriminate against cultures where authority is valued, or against women, who may reason differently from men. Is one stage inherently better than any other? Do the models or the college's program have a liberal bias? Can one teach more effectively by knowing the stages of students? What if the tests show no change? What about the unique goals of each course? All these concerns and more are bound to arise, which is exactly what should happen when faculty use formative assessment to examine student learning and their own teaching goals.

Sprinthall and Thies-Sprinthall (1983) quote extensive studies of inservice education for teachers, which conclude that most are little more than mindless forms of poor entertainment. Their research suggests that faculty development is improved when activities are based on adult developmental stages. They note that theoretically at least, higher-stage teachers are not only more likely to master a variety of models for instruction but also may be more able to choose appropriate models for particular students. Stage growth appears to be best facilitated when a person is guided reflectively in a challenging new role with significant learning potential. At Los Medanos, teaching about and studying one's own and another's development is potentially a significant faculty growth experience.

Conclusion

The search for a framework to guide faculty development in community colleges leads to several basic concepts:

1. Faculty development can no longer be viewed primarily in terms of the individual's subject-matter expertise. It should serve the organizational purpose of promoting excellence in teaching and learning.

2. Personal development, staff development, organizational development, and program development are overlapping processes. Changes in one affect the others; hence, all should be viewed as parts of an interactive learning system.

3. Community colleges are organizational learning systems that rely on a professional drive toward growth, which is fostered through a climate of open dialogue on real, tough problems of teaching and learning.

4. Organizational learning is most effective when it involves key stakeholders.

5. Faculty can learn by doing research on their own practice (for example, assessing the impact of their teaching on the learning process) that simultaneously contributes to the college's learning capacity.

6. Faculty are a community college's single most important slack resource. Without their willingness to learn new skills, the organization has few or no resources available to create new initiatives. Maintaining and building a faculty's skills is an organizationwide imperative.

Clearly, classroom feedback can be an intriguing faculty development tool in widely different college settings. The key to the success of such projects, whether conducted by individuals or groups, is to try to answer the questions that faculty themselves are interested in and to trust their interpretation of the results. In the process of asking and interpreting are the seeds of professional autonomy and self-determination, which are essential to high-quality learning, especially for faculty.

Miami–Dade and Los Medanos effectively illustrate the long-term, large-scale effort involved in developing a learning organization. From pressures for accountability, both institutions reexamined their desired outcomes, developed assessments to better observe current reality, and, with the data that this process produced, recognized serious discrepancies between where they were and where they wanted to be. In both institutions, it was clear that the only resource available to address the gap was the faculty, who would need to be motivated to engage in a major retooling effort. The investment is sizable for such an approach. The results—in terms of student achievement and faculty ability to respond to a changing student population—are worth it.

References

Benveniste, G. *Professionalizing the Organization: Reducing Bureaucracy to Enhance Effectiveness.* San Francisco: Jossey-Bass, 1987.

Bowen, E. "Can Colleges Teach Thinking?" *Time,* February 16, 1987, p. 61.

Boyer, C. M., Ewell, P. T., Finney, J. E., and Mingle, J. R. "Assessment and Outcomes Measurement: A View from the States." *AAHE Bulletin,* March 1987, pp. 8–12.

Chait, R., and Gueths, J. "A Framework for Faculty Development." *Change,* 1981, *13* (4), 30–33.

Cooper, J. *A Paradigm for Staff Development in the Community College.* Elgin, Ill.: National Council for Staff, Program, and Organizational Development, 1984.

Cross, K. P. "Circles, Cycles, and Spirals in the Reform of Higher Education." Paper presented at the Indiana Statewide Faculty Development Conference, Indianapolis, October 31, 1987a.

Cross, K. P. "Restoring Pride and Passion to the Profession of Teaching." Paper presented at the 58th annual conference of the California Association of Community Colleges, Santa Clara, November 21, 1987b.

Halpern, D. F. (ed.). *Student Outcomes Assessment: What Institutions Stand to Gain.* New Directions for Higher Education, no. 59. San Francisco: Jossey-Bass, 1987.

Knefelkamp, L., Widick, C., and Parker, C. A. (eds.). *Applying New Developmental Findings.* New Directions for Student Services, no. 4. San Francisco: Jossey-Bass, 1978.

Kohlberg, L. "Moral Stages and Moralization: The Cognitive-Developmental Approach. In T. Likona (ed.), *Moral Development and Behavior: Theory, Research, and Social Issues.* New York: Holt, Rinehart & Winston, 1976.

Lippitt, G. "Integrating Personal and Professional Development." *Training and Development Journal,* 1980, *24* (5), 34–39.

Perry, W. G., Jr. *Forms of Intellectual and Ethical Development in the College Years.* New York: Holt, Rinehart & Winston, 1968.

Richardson, R. "Staff Development" Address presented to the Summer Conference on Staff Development, sponsored by the National Institute for Staff and Organizational Development and the National Council for Staff, Program, and Organizational Development, Austin, Texas, June 1979.

Saxton, B. "Faculty Renewal: A Model for Professional Development." *Innovation Abstracts,* 1985, 7 (7), 1–2.

Seidman, E. "Merging Access and Excellence: Perspectives on Improving Teaching and Educational Quality." *Community and Junior College Journal,* 1987, 57 (4), 43–45.

Senkpiel, A. "Everyone's Second Choice: Faculty Development at Yukon College." *Innovation Abstracts,* 1986, *8* (24), 1–2.

Sprinthall, N., and Thies-Sprinthall, L. "The Teacher as an Adult Learner: A Cognitive-Developmental View." In G. Griffin (ed.), *Staff Development Eighty-second Yearbook of the National Society for the Study of Education, Part II*. Chicago: University of Chicago Press, 1983.

Wilson, R. C. "Improving Faculty Teaching: Effective Use of Student Evaluations and Consultants." *Journal of Higher Education*, 1986, 57 (2), 196–211.

Zion, C. "Staff Development in the Community College." In W. O'Connell (ed.), *Improving Undergraduate Education in the South*. Atlanta, Ga.: Southern Regional Education Board, 1979.

Sandra C. Acebo is dean of language arts and humanistic studies at Los Medanos College, California. As part of her doctoral program at the University of Texas, she recently completed a semester's internship at Miami–Dade Community College.

Karen Watkins is assistant professor of adult education and human resource development at the University of Texas, Austin. She taught for ten years at Miami–Dade Community College, where she also worked in staff, program, and organizational development. She has worked for the National Institute for Staff and Organizational Development.

*University faculty and school personnel can create partnerships
that serve the dual goals of school improvement and teacher
development.*

Partnerships That Work: Involving Teachers in Their Own Development

Joann Jacullo-Noto

Collaboration between unlike institutions is difficult, even under the
best circumstances. Those who have worked in universities or schools
know this well. Why, then, is there so much renewed interest in university-school partnerships?

The National Commission on Excellence in Education (1983)
sounded the call for school improvement. In the aftermath of its report,
educators in schools and universities began to question what they were
doing wrong that now could be put right. Within three years, two additional reports were issued (Task Force on Teaching as a Profession, 1986;
The Holmes Group, 1986). These reports, along with a Metropolitan
Life Insurance Company survey (1986), spelled out the need to restructure
the teaching profession. To many, the concept of schools and the university joining forces to rethink school improvement and teacher education
made sense. Some viewed this concept as having great appeal. For others,
it was an idea that was already a partial reality through networks that
had been established for school improvement, using many of the traditional approaches to staff and curriculum development.

As Hampel (1988) notes, the history of university-school partner-

V. J. Marsick (ed.). *Enhancing Staff Development in Diverse Settings.*
New Directions for Continuing Education, no. 38. San Francisco: Jossey-Bass, Summer 1988.

64

ships in the late nineteenth and twentieth centuries has been characterized by ambivalence and increasing reliance on third parties as brokers. Problems that have clouded these partnerships include costs and incentives, but both sides can learn from experiments in the 1980s as they respond to the call for renewed collaboration, this time through the creation of professional development schools. Although varying in nature and structure, such schools will have in common the challenge of working with all children, employing professionals who will reach out to the community, and testing alternative roles for college faculty and school personnel.

It is hoped that teachers will develop as leaders while they teach children, and that university faculty will study best practices in collaboration with teachers (Lanier, 1988). The professional development school will be a community of learners and inquirers aimed at school improvement and the reform of teacher education. Linked with this venture is the expectation that schools of education and liberal arts colleges can work together to improve teacher education, both preservice and inservice. Although there are several models in place (Schenly High School, Pittsburgh) and others forming (the Jefferson County Public School/ Gheens Professional Development Academy, Kentucky), most universities are just beginning to question the need for collaboration with schools.

For those who accept this challenge, there are understandings about staff development (Griffin, 1983; Lieberman and Miller, 1984; Little, 1987), school improvement (Lieberman, 1986; Wideen and Andrews, 1987), and teacher education (Zumwalt, 1986; Shulman and Sykes, 1983) on which to reflect as the partnership is conceived and unfolds. There are also important lessons to be learned from recent partnership ventures that differ in structure, scope, and intent from the newly proposed professional development school.

This chapter presents a case study of one model, Interactive Research and Development Schooling (IR&DS), which provided growth opportunities through a university-school partnership. The model grew out of a network of schools, linked to Teachers College at Columbia University, called the Metropolitan School Study Council (MSSC). This model, an alternative to traditional inservice teacher education, provides opportunities for all partners to grow and learn. It suggests a very specific strategy that enables university faculty and school personnel to work together on school issues and problems through a variety of partnership models.

A Research and Development Model for University-School Partnerships

Action Research. This strategy developed as an alternative approach to teacher inservice education in the MSSC, which linked Teachers College with forty-six public school districts in New York, New Jersey, and Connecticut. University faculty need to know the political and social structure of a school or a school district before engaging in a long-term partnership. MSSC both provided that knowledge and established trust. It defined its primary purpose as the nurture and support of member school districts that wished to go beyond minimum educational programs for students and staff development programs for teachers. The member districts have maintained high standards of excellence and innovation. At the same time, the council has provided the college with field sites for student teachers' placement and research. College faculty conduct workshops where school personnel can learn about recent research and faculty can engage in thought-provoking discussions with school teachers and administrators.

The IR&DS model was initiated in MSSC after four years of successful network programs. The notion of collaborative research dates back to the 1940s and early 1950s, when Teachers College emphasized and encouraged the cooperative study of school problems by practitioners and researchers. Lewin (1948) and Lippitt (1949) created useful definitions of cooperative study, which Corey (1953) used to develop action research. Ward and Tikunoff (1982), in their analysis of collaborative research, notes that Corey and others focused on curriculum, while more recent collaborative research has focused on teaching and schooling, but the underlying premises are the same.

IR&DS is based on action research. Each team is composed of a university researcher, a staff developer, and several teachers. Decisions regarding research questions, data-collection procedures, and materials development are researched collaboratively. A "work with" rather than "work on" approach is emphasized. The problem to be studied comes from the school situation. Research and development are concurrent, and the integrity of the classroom is preserved. This process is conceived as a staff development strategy in which rigorous and useful research is also conducted.

This model increases the relevance of research to the real problems and concerns of the teachers involved. Traditional research focuses on questions or problems identified by university researchers outside the school setting. Not only do the problems often have little relevance to classroom life as teachers view it, but teachers also find the reports of these research efforts difficult to read. The language used is that of university researchers, not that of teachers. Compounding the situation is the time lag of approximately eight years between research and the dissemination of findings. Schools, classrooms, and children change, sometimes rapidly, to meet changing social conditions. Another important reason for conceiving of research and development as concurrent processes is to enable teachers to develop their problem-solving capacities by using research methodology.

The Three Teams. The IR&DS project was conceived with several purposes in mind. One goal was to determine the degree of success with which individuals with different backgrounds and professional orientations could fill the roles of developer and researcher. Over a twenty-two month period, three teams—each composed of a researcher, a staff developer, and four to six teachers—worked together on research questions that emanated from the teachers' own school settings. One team was made up of staff from a single suburban school district (SD). Another team consisted of teacher-centered specialists (TC) from the United Federation of Teachers. The third team, in an intermediate agency (IA), consisted of individuals in a variety of positions in a vocational high school. School administrators on two teams served as staff developers. This author served as project director, accessible to the teams but based at the college and supported by staff, who provided technical assistance and documented progress and the project's impact on faculty.

On two teams, the researchers were full-time university professors; a classroom teacher with a doctorate in education served as the researcher on the SD team. The two university professors had briefly been classroom teachers. Both had made their way to the university after securing doctorates and were now professors in the curriculum and teaching department. Although both had worked with teachers and other school personnel on short-term inservice activities, they had not previously worked on a two-year project with a small group of teachers and administrators. Thus, this work with schools was markedly different from their previous school-linked work.

Problem Definition. During the twenty-two months of the project, members of each team identified issues of concern to themselves and their colleagues. These issues were stated as research questions. Each team then developed a research design to study its own question. The SD team decided to study the writing of children in elementary schools. Its question was "How do children perceive, acquire, and apply the principles of good writing?" The TC team studied teachers' job satisfaction in a large urban setting. Its research question was "What are the factors that enable some teachers to maintain positive attitudes about their jobs?" The IA team decided to focus on disruptive students in classrooms, a problem that has always existed but appeared more prominent with the advent of mainstreaming. Its research question was "How can the frequency or severity of disruptive behavior in the classroom be reduced?"

The contribution of the university professors on two teams was crucial at the stage of phrasing research questions, although they also contributed significantly to the discussion of which issues to select for study. They brought examples of research questions to their teams, facilitated discussion of ways to state the questions, and encouraged teams to be clear about the time and effort they could devote to the study of the questions they had selected.

Conflict, Commitment, and Collaboration. Across teams and contexts, researchers were able to identify several themes concerning adult development, particularly conflict, commitment, and collaboration. The data sources through which this information was collected included pre- and postquestionnaires, participants' contact reports, and the logs in which participants wrote weekly entries about the progress of their projects and reactions to the work they were doing. Conflict emerged in all three teams in different ways, often as team members took on new roles that clashed with current professional responsibilities. Several important issues developed concerning the university's role in collaborating with schools. The teachers on the TC team were reluctant to listen to the comments of the university professor on the research problem. They felt they knew schools and what was worth studying. It was difficult for them to separate this knowledge from the phrasing of a research question and the selection of research procedures. As a consequence, the university professor had difficulty getting the attention of the group when she spoke. The team easily became bogged down in discussing research procedures.

The IA team's conflict was not over substance or group process. This team's pattern of conflict centered on the difference between the researcher's view of IR&DS and the team's view. The teachers and the developer, all school practitioners, were interested in solutions to school problems. The researcher wanted to study disruptive students in class, while the teachers wanted to solve the problem. This conflict persisted throughout the project, but it arose only at one or two critical points.

Personal and professional outcomes for teachers were greatly affected as teachers took on leadership roles and researchers and developers became less of a pivotal force on each team. Questions of commitment were raised because of the amount of time and energy required by what was, for most of these practitioners, a first experience of research and development. For example, the teachers on the SD team conducted lunchtime presentations in other elementary schools and at town meetings to explain the project. They became spokespersons for the project and consequently for some of the district's work in the teaching of writing. Teachers said that in the second year they did all the work on their own; in fact, others did participate less frequently, and the team rarely used the consultant that year. At several points, when pressured by other professional and personal commitments, these teachers questioned for whom they were doing the work. Their perceived lack of support caused them to question what benefits they were deriving from this effort, which demanded so much time and energy.

The teacher specialists on the TC team were very much aware

that time devoted to team meetings was time away from their jobs. No substitutes could be secured to do their work because of its very nature. These team members questioned this amount of time, especially when, after meetings, they had to return to their jobs with several hours of work still to be done.

On each of the two teams with university professors, the teacher's view of the professor's professional life frequently was at issue. They believed the professors had more time to engage in research projects and did not face problems of lack of support. In fact, both professors were facing similar issues, since neither was tenured at the time of the project, yet there was no open discussion of tension, although one professor broached this issue later with one member of her team. It is clear that discussion centered on mutual concerns might have served to build bridges between professionals on both sides.

The project identified some of the troublesome issues that arise when institutions with different schedules, reward structures, and purposes come together for their mutual good. For instance, when schedules had to be adjusted, in many cases it was the university project staff who revised them, as requested by the teachers. This often created problems in renegotiating timetables with funders, yet it was clear that the teachers needed time extensions for good reasons. Negotiations between the institutions and the people involved usually centered on who could afford to bend on a particular issue. Throughout the two years of the project, many such questions continued to be raised, suggesting new ways of thinking about how schools and universities could collaborate on research projects.

Reinforcement, Recognition, and Respect. For the university researchers, the question studied by the TC team had far-ranging significance. Anyone concerned with long-range staff development, whether in schools or in universities, has probably attempted to identify the rewards and incentives to which teachers respond most positively. The TC team was able to identify three: reinforcement, recognition, and respect. Results of this team's research indicated that reinforcement from adults (and from students), along with recognition and respect from fellow teachers, administrators, and parents, are essential if teachers are to retain positive attitudes toward their jobs. It also became clear that the university professors, whose work with schools conflicted with their tenure demands, needed the same rewards.

Teachers discovered that the opportunity to participate on an IR&DS team over an extended period of time enabled them to experience reinforcement, recognition, and respect. For example, speaking at faculty meetings, parent association meetings, and national conferences about their research gave these teachers recognition and respect. Members of both the school district and TC teams reported that this project had been an unmatched growth opportunity. The same factors affected faculty satisfaction, but there were key differences, centering on such issues as time (scheduling and allotment of time for discussion), sites for meetings, what the research was, and how much each faculty member had learned from the project. The teachers proclaimed themselves researchers at the close of the project. The university faculty hesitatingly reported new understandings of the school as a workplace and of the nature of teaching in schools. They also felt that the teachers had tried their wings at problem solving but did not yet call them researchers.

Research, Development, and Learning. More specific short- and long-term rewards differed for teacher members of the three teams. Initially, the SD team expected to lean heavily on the university to learn how to do rigorous research. In the end, however, it was actually the teachers who designed the research, collected the data, and wrote the final report. Their rewards emanated from their own new sense of power and authority, as a result of their having done research. One teacher reported, "We now feel we can speak with authority not only on research, but about teaching, about how children learn and also about being professional."

The project gave the teacher specialists on the TC team new status among their peers. More important, they came to see the process and the products of their work to be of prime benefit to teacher centers, to their union, and to themselves. For the IA team, although the vocabulary and the systematic research process was of some benefit, the most powerful rewards came through the opportunity for development. They ended the two-year project with a greater sense of confidence in their own abilities, both to solve problems and to engage their peers in similar processes.

All the teachers involved were questioned, at the beginning and at the end of the project, about their own and their colleagues' interest in various types of staff development activities. One result seemed to be a much stronger interest on the part of the teachers in an exchange of ideas with colleagues at other schools and in professional conferences. Participating teachers also seemed to feel that their colleagues were far less interested in inservice activities than they were. These teachers saw themselves as highly professional and, partly as a result of this experience, spoke of plans for their own continuing professional growth.

Most of the IR&DS teacher participants had entered the project with little knowledge of research and some doubts about how much they would learn. At the end, however, many had learned a great deal and expressed pleasure and a new sense of confidence. A similar tale can be told about development. The TC team set aside small amounts of money to replicate its process with additional teams of teachers and principals in the urban school district. The IA team teachers served as staff developers for the district in a variety of capacities following the project; they believed they had more credibility than outside consultants did. Their realization that development can be process-oriented, rather than product-oriented, was the most dramatic outcome for them.

The Problem-Solving Process. Identifying and acting on perceived problems provided a focus for the teacher-researchers' work in their school districts. The teacher participants were eager to find answers to the questions and problems they had identified. In doing so, they learned from other problems that arose throughout the project. For example, midway through the project, the school district's assistant superintendent announced that the ten released-time days planned for the second year would be reduced to five or fewer. The teams struggled for several meetings with their responses. Should members stop working on their project because the ground rules had been changed? Should they protest, expecting to have the time reinstated? They finally decided to register their disagreement with the decision and press on with project tasks. In another example, a team discussed parents' complaints about the substitutes who had been secured to cover classes while teachers attended team meetings. The team also talked about its own misgivings. Still, it took months for the team to understand this problem in any terms other than "lack of administrative support." Nevertheless, at the close of the project, the teachers on the team reported a new appreciation for the complexity of schools and school life, student differences, teacher preferences, system rules and policies, parental expectations, and curricular demands.

The parallels between the teachers and the university professors were evident, if not always appreciated. University faculty, for example, felt that the reduction in the teachers' released time was unfair, but they expected the teachers simply to proceed with the work, without reflecting on their own reactions to similar situations at the university. The project illustrated that it is not easy to build some bridges between these two worlds.

Impacts on School Districts and the University. There is evidence, too, that the three teams' research and development had impacts on their respective school districts. The SD team developed a method of involving additional district teachers in the writing-process approach. Other teachers in the district have now created a research team to further the work on the study of children's writing. The TC team members created teams similar to their own in eleven other schools.

The changes that took place as a result of the IA team's work were perhaps the most dramatic. The teachers on that team had never done any research before, nor had they been exposed to the products of research. For them, staff development had always taken the form of an outside expert coming in to address an issue. This was becoming, for many, less and less tolerable. Now, with their newfound expertise and confidence, the IA team teachers were willing and eager to be used as peer staff developers. They had, after all, tried out several interventions on a major problem that had been identified by students and teachers. As a result, they had been afforded an opportunity to learn systematic problem solving and at the same time take on the role of teaching other teachers.

The university professors involved in the project were not able to report similar results. Like most similar projects at the university, this one stayed in the domain of the faculty engaged in it. Regular reports on the project were given to the dean and were included in the portfolios of nontenured faculty. A course in action research was designed and initiated by the IR&DS project director, but there has been no other evidence of any impact of the collaborative project on the university that sponsored it.

Reflections on the IR&DS Model

To create partnerships between schools and the university that are complex in scope and design, the partners must have sustained contact with each other over time. This allows the potential partners to get to know each other before entering a high-stakes relationship. In addition, complex projects of short or long duration and involving both institutions are more likely to be created when there are benefits to both. It is clear that the establishment of a network, such as MSSC, can serve as the foundation from which more complex projects, such as the IR&DS project, develop.

There are often benefits for the individuals involved in long-term partnerships. In this instance, as a result of the project, two teachers from the IR&DS teams are enrolled in doctoral programs at the college and one teacher team teaches with the MSSC director in a college class and in MSSC workshops. Two of the three school districts involved in the project have sought further assistance from the college in program development and evaluation. The relationship between the college and the school deepened and expanded as a result of the project. As college faculty interact with teachers and administrators in new structures, such as professional development schools, they may create settings in which they can learn from one another. This may be part of the answer to the question of how to provide staff development to individuals who have been employed in schools and colleges for many years in the same roles.

The Character of the New Partnership

Partnerships between universities and schools are changing. In the past, individuals sought out schools, or schools sought out individuals, for specialized projects. These projects, if initiated by individual faculty members, were often linked to funding received for research and development. If a school sought the partnership, it was often to secure an evaluation of a school program or obtain on-site assistance. These were often topic-specific projects of relatively short duration. Partnerships designed for the 1980s and the 1990s are different in several respects. Those like MSSC, somewhere between the old forms and the soon-to-be created professional development schools, link many schools to a university and involve the pooling of financial and other resources. School members learn from one another, from the faculty at the university, and from other educational leaders their pooled resources now make available. College faculty can conduct research in the network schools. In these new partnerships, each must explore the capacity of the other and then determine which resources are valuable. These partnerships often begin on goodwill, move to a level of initial trust, and then into serious negotiations concerning access to resources.

From the outset, partners become knowledgeable about each other's capacities. The institutions involved have made a calculated decision that each is worthy of the effort. This judgment can be made on a number of bases. A school district can view a potential college partner as having valuable human and material resources, a high status in the profession, and important and timely knowledge to share. The college can view a school district as having the necessary school population it wishes to study or serve, a philosophy of education compatible with that of the college, administrators who understand the process of implementing new programs in schools, and teachers who wish to work collaboratively on a new venture.

New partnerships will often begin with funds from several sources. There may be planning grants secured by a collaborative effort of both school and college faculty, as well as a reallocation of funds by each of the participating partners. New ways of thinking about instruction time and about ways to change schools as workplaces may result. Many individuals are aware that the venture cannot be built solely on external funds. If these collaborative efforts are to succeed, a reallocation of current budgets is required to maintain the partnership over time and signify collaboration and commitment.

One interesting issue for colleges is the need to engage faculty colleagues in the venture. In the MSSC network, two faculty members had prime responsibility for the network, while others were tapped occasionally to interact in limited ways with school personnel. In the partnerships of the future, groups of faculty will need to be directly involved with schools on a continual basis. A good example of this evolution of partnerships is a university-school effort launched by Dartmouth College in 1983. A summer institute, the Computer Literacy and Information Processing Program, was initiated by two faculty members with the support of the dean. It sought to link the college to five urban school districts for inservice education of secondary-level teachers. The institute, conducted annually, has been reshaped, as faculty have learned more about the use of technology and about the training of experienced teachers. In addition, faculty have recognized the need to reach out to teachers, once they are back in their schools, and to provide opportunities for their continued growth and development. They have also identified other college faculty who agree with the philosophy and goals of the program and have something of value to share with those already involved.

Faculty have to get to know one another more than superficially to forge agreements on basic principles before attempting to work with schools. There is a fine line, however, between the internal need of college faculty to agree on what they stand for and the task of deciding what the partnership should look like. This may pose a problem for faculty who want to know the exact nature and scope of the partnership before bringing in other institutions. The same is true for school leaders entering partnerships.

If the new partnerships suggest long-term commitments, there are many hurdles to cross. One problem for teachers and professors alike concerns expected outcomes and the time required to reach them. Teachers may view a partnership as a way to achieve quick solutions to the many problems they face daily in their classrooms, but partnerships require time and may not solve problems quickly. Teachers will need to rethink their time commitments to deal with a process that requires methodical planning, reflective thinking, reevaluation, and often readjustment of project goals. Focusing on process, rather than on product, and slowing down the process are challenging dimensions of the partnership. College faculty also need to be aware of daily and yearly school schedules, to avoid putting pressure on teachers at all the wrong times. Faculty, pressured by work demands, will have to make the time to be in schools. For any professional, it is difficult to move predictably out of one's own workplace and into another with different norms. If teachers and college faculty establish partnerships that serve the goals of the institutions in which they work, it will be easier to make the necessary time commitments.

As groups of college faculty and teachers choose to work closely together, there is the possibility of greater institutionalization of new ways of thinking, teaching, and conducting research.

The professional development model of the 1990s would involve schools and colleges of education and liberal arts in a very public and highly visible working relationship. Often in the past, partnerships were heard of only if they were successful. The new partnerships will be conducted on a large scale, and their success or failure will be known to many. What outcomes will each partner expect from long-term collaboration?

Griffin (1988) notes that people need to work together differently, rather than longer or harder, to make these partnerships succeed. As in any other new venture, there will optimism and promise at the outset. Perhaps this moment of great promise will need to be tempered with realism.

Conclusion

As university faculty create partnerships with schools, perhaps it will be best to follow the advice of Fullan (1987), who suggests that staff development is best served by the promotion of diversity, since not enough is known to recommend one single approach. This is true of university-school partnerships. Partnerships in the past were often forged by individuals who sought out one another, built trust, and began to work together. Partnerships in the 1990s will require more. Each institution must be willing to create personnel and structural arrangements that may go counter to its own structure of rewards and incentives. When each participating institution sees the effort as being in its own best interest, these new collaborative partnerships may accomplish even more than we have hoped.

References

Corey, S. M. *Action Research to Improve School Practice.* New York: Bureau of Publications, Teachers College, Columbia University, 1953.

Fullan, M. "Implementing the Implementation Plan." In M. F. Wideen and I. Andrews (eds.), *Staff Development for School Improvement: A Focus on the Teacher.* New York: Falmer Press, 1987.

Griffin, G. (ed.), *Staff Development.* Chicago: National Society for the Study of Education, 1983.

Griffin, G. Response to keynote address, presented to the national meeting of the Holmes Group, Washington, D.C., January 1988.

Hampel, R. "School-University Partnerships in Historical Perspective." Paper presented to the national meeting of the Holmes Group, Washington, D.C., January 1988.

The Holmes Group. *Tomorrow's Teachers.* East Lansing, Mich.: The Holmes Group, 1986.

Lanier, J. Keynote address presented to the national meeting of the Holmes Group, Washington, D.C., January 1988.

Lewin, K. *Resolving Social Conflicts.* New York: Harper & Row, 1948.

Lieberman, A. (ed.). *Rethinking School Improvement: Research, Craft, and Concept.* New York: Teachers College Press, 1986.

Lieberman, A., and Miller, L. *Teachers, Their World and Their Work: Implications for School Improvement.* Alexandria, Va.: Association for Supervision and Curriculum Development, 1984.

Lippitt, R. *Training in Community Relations: A Research Exploration Toward New Group Skills.* New York: Harper & Row, 1949.

Little, J. W. "Assessing the Prospects for Teacher Leadership." Paper presented to the annual meeting of the American Education Research Association, Washington, D.C., April 1987.

Metropolitan Life Insurance Company. *The American Teacher, 1986: Restructuring the Teaching Profession.* New York: Metropolitan Life Insurance Company, 1986.

National Commission on Excellence in Education. *A Nation at Risk.* Washington, D.C.: U.S. Government Printing Office, 1983.

Shulman, L. S., and Sykes, G. (eds.). *Handbook of Teaching and Policy.* New York: Longman, 1983.

Task Force on Teaching as a Profession. *A Nation Prepared: Teachers for the Twenty-First Century.* New York: Carnegie Forum on Education and the Economy, 1986.

Ward, B. A., and Tikunoff, W. J. "Collaborative Research." Paper presented to the Implications of Research on Teaching for Practice Conference, Washington, D.C., February 1982.

Wideen, M. F., and Andrews, I. (eds.). *Staff Development for School Improvement: A Focus on the Teacher.* New York: Falmer Press, 1987.

Zumwalt, K. (ed.). *Improving Teaching.* Alexandria, Va.: Association of Supervision and Curriculum Development, 1986.

Joann Jacullo-Noto has served as director of the IR&DS project. Her recent work for the Sherman Fairchild Foundation concerns mathematics and the use of technology by experienced teachers in six major cities in the United States. She is currently director of teacher education at Teachers College, Columbia University, and director of the Metropolitan School Study Council (MSSC).

*To eliminate staff burnout in social service agencies, managers
must acquire deeper understanding of the problem and take
a more active role in prevention.*

Developing Managers
to Prevent Staff Burnout

Gloria Pierce

Healing the Healers

Although burnout is not the focus of as much attention as it was
in the 1970s, the problem itself is at least as severe as it was then, especially in social service agencies. Social service agencies have been stunned
in the 1980s by a plethora of increasingly virulent social plagues—the
crack crisis, the AIDS epidemic, an increasing incidence of adolescent
suicide and child abuse, high rates of alcoholism and abuse of other
drugs, to mention just a few. Ironically and unfortunately, when business
is booming in the social service system, it means that society is hurting.
Eventually, social service workers and their organizations also start to
hurt. The urgency of burnout reflects the awareness that society's healers
are themselves in need of healing.

Staff development in social service agencies can play a key role in
addressing burnout, not only by providing training about the issue but
also by developing managers who create a climate in the organization that
empowers staff to help themselves before they burn out. This chapter
describes burnout and its causes. It explores staff development dilemmas
and solutions to burnout, focusing primarily on management development,
and concludes with an approach recommended for social service agencies.

V. J. Marsick (ed.). *Enhancing Staff Development in Diverse Settings.*
New Directions for Continuing Education, no. 38. San Francisco: Jossey-Bass, Summer 1988.

This chapter draws on the author's experience in a nonprofit corporation in New York City that provides research and training services to treatment centers, clinics, therapeutic communities, hospitals, government agencies, and nonprofit organizations concerned with the prevention and treatment of substance abuse. This training institute functions as a consultant to social service systems, offering programs for staff in all areas and at all organizational levels. Most services of this institute are delivered to public-sector or nonprofit clients who are social service providers.

Burnout is psychic and physical exhaustion caused by severe depletion of an individual's resources. He or she cannot restore energy under stressful conditions over an extended period. When the syndrome affects entire systems, it is known as staff burnout. Selye (1974) has suggested that prolonged exposure to a stressor that cannot be removed or adequately dealt with eventually results in the organism's exhaustion and death.

In the earlier stages of burnout, the system is better able to resist and cope with stress, because its reserves of energy are less depleted. Administrative and managerial intervention and prevention efforts have a greater chance of success when made at the first signs of burnout. In the earlier stages, workers seem to exert more effort to accomplish less. In the later stages, employees attempt to minimize contact with clients, the work, and the organization by taking extended lunches and coffee breaks, codifying and formalizing roles and relationships, and withdrawing and isolating themselves (physically, psychologically, or both), from co-workers and clients.

The organizational climate is characterized by apathy, mistrust, and disrespect manifested by intergroup conflicts, protection of organizational "turf," poor vertical and lateral communication, and the acting out of negative feelings toward authority. Vital links and relationships with other agencies and the community often become strained.

Causes of Burnout

Because burnout is a pervasive, systemic phenomenon, it is clear that its cure is not simply a dose of training. Staff development must be considered as an organizational, systemic intervention. Hence, before any discussion of solutions to burnout, it is essential to grasp the complex interaction of the many factors that contribute to the problem including cultural values, personal attributes, the nature of the work, working conditions, and organizational characteristics.

Cultural Values. Our collective overemphasis on material possessions and technology has reduced staff members' ability to be gratified by the small, simple rewards that counteract burnout. Inflated expectations generate nebulous but powerful undercurrents of dissatisfaction, provoking a search for the big payoff that always eludes us (Freudenberger, 1980). Related to the pursuit of grandeur is tacit approval or even open admiration accorded to workaholics, while the underlying pathology and negative consequences of workaholism escape scrutiny. In this way, an abundance of candidates for burnout is ensured.

Another cultural value that contributes to burnout is our enchantment with technology. Western civilization operates from the belief that anything can be done or fixed in an alloted (preferably short) amount of time, and it is easy to forget that the work of healing people is not amenable to this technological model. Nevertheless, the model is all too often inappropriately (if unconsciously) applied to the helping professions. Its practitioners feel an undue sense of failure, guilt, and lessened self-esteem at not being able to accomplish what is expected of a "competent" person in society.

Personal Attributes. Persons attracted to the helping professions often have certain values, tendencies, and personality traits that may predispose them to burnout. Many have a sense of mission and justice, and a desire to make the world a better place for everyone by easing the pain of troubled clients or working for social causes. They are "compassionate and caring, which makes them especially vulnerable to the excessive demands made on them" (Freudenberger, 1980, p. 159). The danger is even greater when their sense of self-worth is tied to their efforts to help others: Staff often feel that they should be able to change the world, or else they are worth nothing.

As might be expected, the helping professions attract many people who have learned to see themselves as saviors or rescuers of others, as the strong person on whom others depend. To complicate matters further, dichotomous thinking may shut out the possibility that sometimes saviors themselves need saving, that the strong person may also need help. The world is perceived as composed of two types of people—those who need and receive care, and those who take care of others. This faulty assumption leads to denial of one's own needs for nurturance and an inability to request or accept assistance or support from others. This particular type of emotional isolation creates pluralistic ignorance, a belief that everyone else is handling the job with confidence, competence, ease, and grace. It then seems best to keep one's own doubt, weariness, confusion, or fear hidden.

Nature of the Work. The nature of the work itself is a great source of stress for the helping professional, whose daily client contact is with the most deprived, depressed, and alienated members of society. A helper's task is essentially to heal those in need. It is emotional labor, in the most profound sense of the phrase. The work of healing requires a caring, attentive presence that is difficult to maintain. If replenishment is not forthcoming, the work eventually exhausts anyone's capacity to give.

In the business world, results are usually quite evident, and there is a sense of completion about the work. The books are balanced, the program or equipment operates, items are produced and sold in the marketplace. In social services, there is seldom a sense of clarity or closure. Failure is frequent. Clients leave treatment or do not respond, despite workers' best efforts. Results are subjective and difficult to measure. Such uncertainty and ambiguity deprive the worker of a clear sense of mastery, competence, and achievement. Succinctly stated, the elusiveness of success causes stress.

Finally, responsibility for the welfare of others is in itself stressful. Surgeons and air traffic controllers, for example, experience a high incidence of stress-related disease (Kahn, 1978). Likewise, social service workers know that their mistakes can affect the well-being of other people.

Working Conditions. Working conditions in the public and nonprofit domains can be especially productive of stress. In general, the physical environment is functional, at best; esthetics is never a high priority. Clinics and treatment facilities are often in neglected, squalid neighborhoods, sometimes in dilapidated buildings. Inadequate budgets force overcrowding. Sharing an office with half a dozen or more colleagues makes it impossible to function optimally. Substandard telephone systems, lack of up-to-date computer technology, and caseloads that are too large contribute to working conditions that would be considered intolerable in private companies but are simply accepted as the norm in many social service agencies.

The misuse or misdistribution of scarce resources adds to the hardships of the already difficult work of human contact. One registered nurse supplied bandages for a clinic from her own personal finances for several months, and such stories are not uncommon. Many nonprofit agencies rent space from slumlords, who fail to maintain the basic facilities.

Finally, low salaries and paltry benefits preclude the amenities that could alleviate stress. Low salaries are matched by the public's attitude toward "social workers." The public is willing to pay just enough to keep social problems at bay, and those who work in the social service system are accorded the same grudging acknowledgment. The very existence of social service workers can be an unpleasant reminder of social problems, which evoke the public's guilt and anxiety.

Organizational Characteristics. A colleague once remarked, "It's pretty difficult to remain a healthy person in a sick organization." Staff in social service agencies are generally underpaid, underappreciated, overworked, and overstressed. Organizational climate contributes more than any other factor to staff burnout. Even more important, it can either exacerbate or ameliorate all other contributing causes.

Organizational structures contribute to burnout. Systems are characterized by work overload, too much direct client contact, inadequate support systems, poor supervision, barriers to the attainment of goals and needs satisfaction, and lack of training and opportunity for advancement. Agencies "tacitly encourage turnover by failing to devise career ladders" (Daley, 1979, p. 26). Feeling stuck or trapped in a job one has outgrown forces the person who cares about professional development to leave the organization.

Although tangible and psychological incentives are minimal, there is still an unspoken expectation of complete dedication. Often, the lack of a well-defined mission, of clear direction, and of an operating plan increases the work load, because the agency commits staff and resources it does not have to activities it should not be doing. As a result, "saving the world" actually becomes employees' job description.

The "good child," who learned always to help and give to others "unselfishly" and without complaint can easily find that familiar role in a social service organization. Essentially, the organization colludes with individuals to support their belief systems about who they are and what they should do: They should endure deplorable conditions and low wages in order to help others, and they should not feel deprived or angry, because they should be able to take it. Offering this kind of insecurity, however, is probably not the agency's best strategy for delivering high-quality service to clients.

Manager Development for Prevention

Many courses are available to teach staff how to manage stress and prevent burnout. If training is provided only to those under stress, however, it is itself part of the problem, because it blames the victims by placing responsibility for failure squarely on employees and ignores the role of the organization in the complex interaction of the causes. Management plays a central role in orchestrating the ways in which contributing factors play themselves out. Hence, effective staff development should start first with management.

Management Training. The initial step in preventing burnout is to design and deliver manager training programs that help managers recognize and own the part they play in the problem. Manager development can both address specific causes of burnout and raise the general level of competence and leadership, so that effective solutions can be discovered and implemented.

Manager development often encounters formidable obstacles. In the private sector, manager education has become rather firmly established. In larger corporations, especially, managers at all levels have become accustomed to training, sometimes on a residential basis. In social service systems, however, training typically is regarded as a skill-building activity for line staff (counselors, nurses, and so forth). Higher-level administrative directors are particularly resistant, perhaps because they believe, as do many of their counterparts in business and industry, that training is an admission of ignorance about matters with which they should already be familiar.

Manager development in social service settings suffers from the same problems that permeate the rest of the system. The relatively low pay offered to adjunct faculty makes it difficult to attract, develop, and retain qualified trainers. Allocations for such training tools as audio-visual equipment, tapes, films, reprints of articles, and notebooks are minimal. Because private industry is the largest market for training films and tapes, most dramatized case studies and examples are more relevant to the business world. Nevertheless, because films can be a powerful shared group experience, they are one of the most effective methods of ensuring continuity and quality and of making courses less dependent on trainers.

Training programs should not suggest that burnout can be prevented by a "bag of tricks"; rather, they should engage managers in an effort to find systemwide solutions aimed at the "elimination of the sources of job-related stress and the provision of mechanisms that . . . allow workers to recoup their energies" (Daley, 1979, p. 22). This effort entails identifying relevant stressors as well as sources of replenishment. Managerial intervention should include "changes in structure, policies and operating procedures of the organization in order to mitigate or eliminate stresses emanating from the work environment" (Carroll, 1979, p. 192).

A Climate for Learning and Growth. Because managers create an organizational climate in which burnout is either fueled or fought, burnout can be viewed as a symptom of mismanagement. In some cases, managers themselves become primary sources of stress for employees.

Herzberg (1968) suggests that staff development involves both motivating and hygiene factors. Hygiene factors satisfy basic needs—for example, salary, job security, or relationships with subordinates, supervisors, and peers. Their presence removes detriments to performance but only brings the employee to a point at which there is no longer dissatisfaction. By contrast, motivating factors satisfy higher-level needs: challenging work, professional growth, and recognition for accomplishments. Job content is the vehicle for satisfaction; elements in the job context merely eliminate impediments to performance. Managers must help staff meet both sets of needs to avoid burnout.

Rausch (1978) provides a framework for a healthy climate, and tools to achieve it. He suggests that there is a need for congruence between individual and organizational goals. With congruence, the organization gains in performance, and the individual gains in needs satisfaction, growth, and well-being. Congruence can be achieved by "linking elements": communications, coaching, counseling, and ensuring that appropriate rewards, both tangible and psychological, are received.

Albrecht (1978) proposes management by objectives precisely to avoid the burnout that results from unclear, unrealistic, imposed goals and expectations: "Disillusionment is a certain indication of one fatal mistake: unrealistic expectations. And the higher the expectations, the more bitter the disillusionment" (p. 24).

Unclear organizational goals generate frustration and divert energy into nonproductive behavior. As one staff member commented, "If you don't know where the goalposts are, why run?" The obstacles to goal attainment become the focus of attention, rather than the goals themselves. In the attempt to feel better about their failure to achieve, workers spend their time in mutual commiseration and other counterproductive activities.

Management by objectives is based on the premise that "the manager's job . . . is to show [people] what has to be accomplished and to help them accomplish it" (Albrecht, 1978, p. 12). The manager can create a climate in which employees can derive rewards by directing their efforts toward the success of the enterprise. This method entails collaborating and agreeing on realistic, attainable goals, prioritizing activities according to payoff, and acknowledging and rewarding goal attainment through performance appraisal.

A Staff Development Approach

These ideas of Herzberg, Rausch, and Albrecht, while not new themselves, form a conceptual framework for an approach that goes beyond but includes training. Good management and a healthy organizational climate are the keys. This approach also addresses the complex, interactive causes of burnout.

Designing Social Service Work. Managers can both counteract and compensate for the nature of social service work in several ways. First, work can be structured to allow as much closure as possible on each case or job assignment. Jobs can be enriched to increase challenges and satisfaction. At times, jobs should also be rotated to allow for growth and easing of stress. In other words, overload and underload should be avoided, both quantitatively and qualitatively (Blanchard and Tager, 1985, pp. 56–58).

Second, given the ambiguity of social service work, managers can help employees set goals that are realistic, attainable, and as meaningful as possible, so that employees can better recognize their own successes. Goals should serve both organizational and individual needs and provide for growth-enhancing assessments. Clarity and feedback are the keys. Amorphous job descriptions should be sharpened and limits set, so that employees do not feel guilty and frustrated when they fail to accomplish what they should never have attempted. Through coaching and counseling, managers can help reformulate stressful problems, so that employees will approach them realistically and not expect too much from themselves, their clients, or their work.

Questioning Cultural, Personal, and Organizational Belief Systems. Both in training sessions and in less formal learning interactions with managers, staff should be helped to uncover assumptions they have taken for granted, air them, and challenge them—for example, the workaholic ideal, the technological model, the savior myth, or the "good child" role. The unconscious belief that one must give to everyone else, take care of everyone else, and save everyone else in order to justify one's existence is an irrational idea, certainly; nevertheless, on the emotional level, it is very real and influences choices and behavior (Ellis and Harper, 1974). Based on old assumptions, which are remnants from childhood, such belief systems are dysfunctional in adult life (Gould, 1978) and should be reevaluated against present-day reality.

Trainers can help staff name taboos and see how their perceptions have been formed by social or cultural forces and reevaluate them. Supervisors can help staff discover feelings about clients and work, can give staff "permission" to have those feelings, and can help staff own them, so that they do not become exaggerated and spill over into other relationships in the agency.

At times, staff may also need to develop an attitude of detached concern, based on the paradoxical principle that one must "distance oneself from people in order to help or cure them" (Pines and Maslach, 1978, p. 239). This attitude can help staff understand their own needs, limits, and vulnerabilities and commit themselves to taking care of themselves as a prerequisite to caring for others. This is the core issue in burnout prevention.

Separating Private and Professional Life. Freudenberger (1975) and White (1978) agree that social service workers should avoid one characteristic of people who have a sense of mission: making their lives one big staff meeting. Staff development typically discourages the inclusion of personal activities in a professional development plan. In social services, however, these activities are essential for rejuvenation. Lippitt (1982) acknowledges the interdependence of professional and personal life but advocates balancing career identity and social identity in ways that enhance self-integration and quality of life (pp. 184–187). Managers can model this behavior themselves by placing limits on staff time at work and guarding against overinvolvement. Pines and Maslach (1978), Kahn (1978), Bryan (1981), Freudenberger (1974), Carroll (1979), White (1978), and O'Toole (1985) all recommend establishing a norm of guilt-free time away from work.

Developing Organizational Rewards and Support. While interesting work can be motivating, managers must also pay attention to hygiene factors that can be demotivating. Working conditions that cannot be changed can at least be acknowledged, but empty platitudinous encouragement will cause staff to wonder, "If I'm so valuable, why am I underpaid, overworked, and unrecognized?"

Despite the limits of bureaucracy, some policies, structures, and practices can be established to nurture, reward, and support staff. It is not enough to assume that employees know they are appreciated. Scarce resources may preclude granting tangible monetary rewards, but recognition and affirmation cost nothing (Bellman, 1986, pp. 43–44; Blanchard and Tager, 1985, pp. 147–153).

Managers may also be able to provide opportunities for training that contribute to career development, guard against "professional incest" (White, 1978) by exposing practitioners to perspectives from outside the agency, and interrupt monotonous routines. O'Toole (1985) advises managers to avoid burnout through "career-long training" (p. 115), "working sabbaticals" (a form of job rotation), and "personal growth sabbaticals" (p. 124).

The obsession with control characterizes bureaucracy and puts workers in a double bind: They are treated like children but are expected to perform like adults with their clients. Administrative controls should be reassessed and replaced. Finally, while maintaining key links with the community, funding sources, and other organizations, agencies must manage their external boundaries to protect staff and resources from being overcommitted.

References

Albrecht, K. *Successful Management by Objectives.* Englewood Cliffs, N.J.: Prentice-Hall, 1978.

Bellman, G. "The Quest for Staff Leadership." *Training and Development Journal,* 1986, *40* (3), 34–36.

Blanchard, M., and Tager, M. *Working Well: Managing for Health and High Performance.* New York: Simon & Schuster, 1985.

Bryan, W. "Preventing Burnout in the Public Interest Community." *The Grantsmanship Center News,* March/April, 1981.

Carroll, J. "Staff Burnout as a Form of Ecological Dysfunction." *Contemporary Drug Problems,* 1979, *8* (22), 185–195.

Daley, M. "Burnout: Smoldering Problem in Protective Services." *Social Work,* 1979, *24* (5), 375–379.

Ellis, A., and Harper, R. *A Guide to Rational Living.* North Hollywood, Calif.: Wilshire Book Company, 1974.

Freudenberger, H. J. "Staff Burnout." *Journal of Social Issues,* 1974, *30* (1), 159–165.

Freudenberger, H. J. *The Staff Burnout Syndrome.* Washington, D.C.: Drug Abuse Council, 1975.

Freudenberger, H. J. *Burnout: The High Cost of High Achievement.* New York: Bantam, 1980.

Gould, R. *Transformations: Growth and Change in Adult Life.* New York: Simon & Schuster, 1978.

Herzberg, F. "One More Time: How Do You Motivate Employees?" *Harvard Business Review,* 1968, *46* (1), 53–62.

Kahn, R. "Job Burnout Prevention and Treatment." *Public Welfare,* 1978, *18* (2), 61–63.

Lippitt, G. *Organizational Renewal.* Englewood Cliffs, N.J.: Prentice-Hall, 1982.

O'Toole, J. *Vanguard Management.* New York: Berkley, 1985.

Pines, A., and Maslach, C. "Characteristics of Staff Burnout in Mental Health Settings." *Hospital & Community Psychiatry,* 1978, *29* (4), 233–237.

Rausch, E. *Balancing Needs of People and Organizations: The Linking Elements Concept.* Cranford, N.J.: Didactic Systems, 1978.

Selye, H. *Stress Without Distress.* New York: Lippincott, 1974.

White, W. "Incest in the Organizational Family: The Unspoken Issue in Staff and Program Burnout." Paper presented to the National Drug Abuse Conference, Seattle, April 1978.

Gloria Pierce is the management development specialist at Narcotic and Drug Research, Incorporated, Training Institute in New York City, where she designs and delivers manager education programs for social service providers throughout the state.

*Corporations, using alternate delivery systems for training, can
meet the need for timely and cost-effective professional
development.*

Training Through Video Teleconferencing: A Corporate Case Study

Linda Shatzer

This chapter explores the use of video teleconferences to take training to
the learners at their worksites. The setting is a large communications
company with offices nationwide. The employees to be trained are all
trainers, but they work with a wide range of staff interests: sales, engi-
neering, management, and support.

The literature on teleconferencing is part of the larger field of
distance learning, which has focused primarily on correspondence courses
and other traditional forms of learning. Researchers are just beginning
to look at the new technologies. Currently, new journals devoted to distance learning are being created in the United States and Canada (for
example, the *American Journal of Distance Education*). Early research
predominantly dealt with behavioral change in environments without
face-to-face interaction (Short, Williams, and Christie, 1975; Finn, 1983).

In business, video teleconferencing has been primarily used as an
alternative to in-person meetings. Often, these types of meetings result in
networks and create better communication in organizations (Rice, 1982).
Only recently, however, has teleconferencing been studied to determine
its effectiveness as an educational delivery system. Such studies have been
conducted in academic environments (Bruyere, 1982).

V. J. Marsick (ed.). *Enhancing Staff Development in Diverse Settings.*
New Directions for Continuing Education, no. 38. San Francisco: Jossey-Bass, Summer 1988.

Development of Teleconferencing Model

This chapter describes the development of an experimental video teleconferencing series, showing how each phase was improved on the basis of evaluation and feedback. It concludes with recommendations for others who wish to experiment with this model.

The organization that planned the video teleconferencing was a corporate training-support group. This group worked with over twenty-seven different internal training organizations, such as those involved in sales and network operations, to identify topics of interest for a teleconferencing series. The support group conducted a needs analysis and synthesized the results on the basis of consensus to arrive at the selected topics. To assist with technical planning, a partnership was established with an internal studio. Arrangements were also made to reserve time on a company-owned satellite to broadcast the programs.

The support group and the technical group met to look at the collected list of suggested topics and to select five: training and human resource development, evaluation, human performance technology, advanced instructor skills, and accelerated learning. Each topic became the subject of a separate teleconferencing session.

Session 1: Training and Human Resource Development

The first teleconference provided an overview of the series and focused on the need for professional development of employees and on the corporation's commitment to developing these programs. It was timed for 2:00 P.M. EST, to allow West Coast personnel to view the program at an acceptable hour. The vice-president for human resources was selected as the guest speaker. His participation clearly conveyed the company's commitment. In addition, employees nationwide could telephone questions to the originating studio, be answered by the vice-president, and comment on his responses.

Technical preparation took place about a month before the teleconference. The corporation had the advantage of already owning and occupying office buildings with rooms equipped to receive satellite signals. Coordinators were available at each site to help employees who attended the presentation. The site coordinators' responsibility was to verify that the satellite signal was being received, take attendance, and send evaluation forms to the project manager.

The signal originated from the site of the live broadcast, a large auditorium. Television cameras sent the signal to a satellite owned by the corporation. Personnel at the site included a television crew, a satellite crew, operators to answer the telephone when employees called in, and a project manager to coordinate activity. Over twenty-five employees called in with questions. The teleconference took two hours.

Figure 1. Teleconferencing Evaluation Form

Please tell us the degree to which you agree or disagree with each of the statements below. Circle the appropriate number, using the scale.

1 = Strongly disgree (*SD*)
2 = Disagree (*D*)
3 = Uncertain (*U*)
4 = Agree (*A*)
5 = Strongly Agree (*SA*)

Content	SD	D	U	A	SA
1. The content of the teleconference was relevant to me.	1	2	3	4	5
2. I can use this information on my job.	1	2	3	4	5
3. I would be interested in another presentation on this topic.	1	2	3	4	5
4. For me, this teleconference was an effective way to receive information.	1	2	3	4	5
5. Questions raised by participants were answered adequately.	1	2	3	4	5

Technical Issues					
6. The video quality was good.	1	2	3	4	5
7. The audio quality was good.	1	2	3	4	5
8. The text images presented were easy to read.	1	2	3	4	5

General Issues					
9. I would life to participate in other teleconferences.	1	2	3	4	5
10. I would recommend this teleconferencing session to others.	1	2	3	4	5

Optional: Name: _________________ Telephone number: _______________

Suggestions for future topics/speakers:

The form displayed in Figure 1 was used for evaluation. Feedback showed scores of about 4.5 for content. (Some technical areas, such as use of text image, were not relevant to this teleconference.) The cost for the use of satellite time was $1,500 per hour. Other costs—personnel, use of the television studio, and materials preparation—were part of internal operating expenses and were charged to the company.

Exact costs will be determined by the internal organization providing the service. In any event, the apparent high costs of satellite-delivered training must be compared to the costs of traditional classroom instruction. There are savings in transportation and time away from the job. Most important, teleconferencing is better than no training at all. Teleconferencing is cost-effective when it replaces traditional training (Lazer, Elton, and Johnson, 1983).

Session 2: Evaluation

The speaker on evaluation had to be both an expert in the field and a good speaker. Donald Kirkpatrick was selected. Dr. Kirkpatrick was well known in the training community for his four-stage evaluation model. The first stage of his model concerns trainees' reactions to training. The second stage involves demonstrations of learning. The third stage includes observation of skills' having been transferred to the workplace. The fourth stage focuses on results, or on how outputs reflect the impact of training (Kirkpatrick, 1967).

Dr. Kirkpatrick had never participated in a teleconference before. The project manager prepared him for the differences between classroom and remote instruction. Dr. Kirkpatrick had to visualize his audience and anticipate questions, especially since there could be no verification by follow-up from remote participants to show that questions had been fully answered (Chute, 1982). Slides were created to illustrate the four-stage evaluation model, and it was important to make them visually interesting.

In the first teleconference, a professional television crew had assisted in the production. In the second session, because the speaker was external to the company, a different approach was taken. The company's own television production studio handled technical presentation, a pattern that was continued for the remaining teleconferences. About a month before the teleconference, flyers were sent out announcing the teleconference and providing information about the thirty-five training sites that would receive the broadcast. The flyers also identified the project manager, who could be contacted with questions. Each location had a coordinator who assisted in the delivery of training. Site coordinators provide points of contact to solve technical difficulties (Minnesota Extension Service, 1987).

To make the presentation more interactive, Dr. Kirkpatrick stopped after discussing each of the four levels of his evaluation model and asked questions of the studio audience. The remote audience also called in questions at this time. Before the teleconference, handouts corresponded to the slides that Dr. Kirkpatrick used as part of his presentation. This teleconference, like the first one, lasted two hours.

Evaluation of this teleconference was generally favorable, even though some of the sites initially lost the signal for fifteen minutes. All sites were telephoned when the problem occurred. Many employees became impatient and decided not to stay, but others allowed for the interruption and remained with the presentation. More than one hundred employees were in the "live" viewing audience. Videotapes of this presentation, at last calculation, had been viewed by another hundred or so employees, and there have been many requests for handouts and bibliographical references. The studio audience reacted well to the higher level of interaction, but some viewers found it confusing. As a result, the planning committee decided to have one hour of presentation followed by one hour of questions, as in the first teleconference. Evaluations of the second session were used in planning for the third.

Session 3: Human Performance Technology

The speaker on human performance technology was George Geis, of McGill University. This topic was selected because of the increasingly important role of performance technologists, who diagnose performance deficiencies and make recommendations for solutions. Since the presence of performance technologists is relatively new, the presentation by Dr. Geis provided an overview of their role.

To prepare for the third teleconference, a larger system for publicity was established. Informal feedback from the first two teleconferences indicated that not all employees were aware of the series. Therefore, visibility was increased through internal publications, a major story in the company newsletter, and direct mail to the two hundred instructional technologists in the company. Site coordinators were asked to display flyers announcing the teleconference. Results of the publicity were measured in the evaluation.

The delivery of the human performance teleconference had no technical problems, but fewer people attended the live broadcast. Part of the reason for the smaller size of the audience may have been that this teleconference was broadcast on a Friday afternoon. The topic also did not appeal to as large an audience as had been expected. Dr. Geis presented a fifty-minute lecture accompanied by slides. After the lecture, call-in questions were read by a moderator, who had introduced and would later sum up the program.

Despite the smaller audience, Dr. Geis was well rated as an expert and a speaker. In some locations, however, equipment malfunctioned. In other locations, the rooms that had been reserved were being used for other activities. Increased awareness of the program apparently had no effect for videocassettes. In fact, at some locations the whole series of videotapes is being used for staff development. While this was not the original intention, this use of videos has expanded the effects of the program. Overall, the teleconference was successful, and there was a recommendation to try a panel format to increase interactivity in the remaining teleconferences.

Session 4: Advanced Instructor Skills

One of the original target audiences for the teleconferencing series was the instructors in the company, and so the topic of advanced instructor skills was selected. Once again, the broadcast was delivered on the first Friday of the month at 2:00 P.M. EST. Wilbert McKeachie, of the University of Michigan, was the speaker.

Dr. McKeachie, unlike the previous two speakers, had appeared on television before, although never in a teleconference. Aware of the program's need for interactivity, he included exercises for the viewing audience to complete and asked viewers to write down questions in advance, which could then be called in to the program. Evaluation showed that this technique had worked well. A panel of experts was chosen to question and comment on the points being raised. The moderator was Dr. Charles F. Martinetz, an expert from the corporation in the area of instructor delivery skills; Stephanie Donato of Rutgers University and Sonja Eveslage of Edison College contributed to the discussion as members of the panel.

Dr. McKeachie spoke for fifty minutes and then asked for questions. The moderator of the panel facilitated discussion by reading the questions called in by the viewing audience and then allowing panel members to offer opinions and comments. As a result of this change in technique, many more questions were raised by both the remote and the studio audiences. At the end of the second hour, Dr. McKeachie's book *Teaching Tips*, was recommended, and information about obtaining the book was put on the television screen. Participants in the studio audience were given complimentary copies of the book, signed by Dr. McKeachie.

According to the evaluation, this teleconference was the most successful. The remote audience apparently needed to be reminded that they were in a two-way, interactive environment and could ask questions (Kenda, 1984). Before the broadcast, all the sites were tested to prevent technical difficulties, and none occurred. Telephone requests for more information about Dr. McKeachie's book illustrate the impact of this program on viewers: They wanted more information. As before, evaluation provided feedback and resulted in suggestions for the next broadcast.

On the basis of this teleconference's evaluation, four major improvements were adopted. Organizers decided to remind the viewing audience to write down and ask questions, use a panel of experts to increase interactivity, provide a host to introduce the speaker and facilitate discussion with the panelists, and extend the learning experience through electronic mail.

Session 5: Accelerated Learning

A technique originally used in Europe, accelerated learning is reputed to increase retention of learning and reduce instructional time. The use of baroque music and guided visual imagery are among its techniques. The speaker for this teleconference was David Meier, director of the Accelerated Learning Institute in Lake Geneva, Wisconsin.

Publicity began a month in advance, with flyers, newsletter announcements, and an article in the company's journal. Educational conferences offered through the company also provided interested participants with information on the upcoming teleconference. Martinetz was asked to moderate again. Again, a panel of experts was selected, and included Charlotte Foster, a consultant who uses accelerated learning in training programs, and Alan Cohen, a manager of electronic training systems, an area where accelerated learning is currently being applied.

Several changes in format were made. After the title credits, the moderator welcomed the viewing audience, explained the role of the remote audience, and reminded both groups to ask questions. Next, the moderator introduced the panel and the guest speaker. The speaker lectured, showed a short video and slides, and provided exercises for the viewing audience. He ended by asking the audience to write down and call in questions. The moderator then asked the panelists to raise questions from their own areas of expertise and balanced those questions with questions from the live and remote audiences. At the end of the program, the panel's expert on electronic training systems explained how participants could continue their dialogue with the speaker and with one another by using electronic mail; a month of follow-up computer conferences provides continuing education.

This time, only one site had technical difficulties. Evaluation of this program showed high satisfaction with content and presentation.

Recommendations

The corporation will continue its teleconference series, because it believes the series is cost-effective and provides opportunities for professional development to the training community. Unanticipated outcomes included the popularity of the videotapes for continued learning and a large number of unknown participants, who have become aware of the series and are requesting satellite dishes to receive its signal. Locations that have fewer training programs than other parts of the company have become the largest constituency.

Once teleconferencing facilities are available, the following recommendations will help organizations plan similar programs:

1. There must be a high level of management support and financial commitment to the project.
2. A human resource group should act as an advocate to provide professional development to employees through teleconferencing.

3. There must be an adequate number of trained personnel to support technical functions.
4. A committee must be set up to select topics and speakers.
5. A project manager must be available to direct selection, publicity, site coordinators, delivery of the teleconferences, and the technical committee.
6. An evaluation system is needed to measure the effectiveness and efficiency of the program.

Conclusion

Many major corporations are currently using satellite technology to deliver training. Their success has depended on the principles suggested by the six recommendations discussed here. Further work needs to be done on determining the most appropriate instructional design for teleconferencing. Widner (1986) suggests the use of timely topics, interactivity between speaker and viewing audience, and video-based enhancement of visuals. Another major issue concerns ways to measure the transfer and application of information back to the work environment.

In the corporation discussed here, the use of electronic systems for staff development has proved to be a workable alternative to classroom instruction. Increased competition and globalization of the marketplace have prompted corporations to use teleconferencing for the delivery of information (Keller and Cross, 1985). Educational teleconferences have recently become more popular (Girishankar, 1987). As an alternative to classroom instruction, teleconferencing can reach a geographically dispersed training audience, without requiring a great deal of travel. Another benefit is its immediacy. In a competitive environment, immediate training on new products is a high priority. Other types of training that require long development make teleconferencing a preferable alternative. In addition, teleconferencing can be linked to other technologies, such as computer conferencing (Shatzer, 1987). Provisions for technical facilities are complex, however, and the corporation's commitment of human and material resources must be strong for this type of staff development to be successful.

References

Bruyere, S. "The Use of Telecommunications Technology in Training of Rehabilitation Personnel." *Journal of Rehabilitation,* 1982, *48,* 60–64.

Chute, A. "Selecting Appropriate Strategies for Training Teleconference Presenters." *Teleconferencing and Electronic Communications,* 1982, *6,* 299–302.

Finn, A. "Process and Structure in Computer-Mediated Group Communication." Unpublished doctoral dissertation, Washington University, Missouri, 1983.

Girishankar, S. "Distance Learning Gathering Steam as a Method for Reaching Smaller Schools Through Teleconferencing." *Communications Week,* May 25, 1987, 44–46.

Keller, K., and Cross, T. *Teleconferencing: Linking People Together Electronically.* Englewood Cliffs, N.J.: Prentice-Hall, 1985.

Kenda, W. "International Teleconferencing." In L. Parker and C. Olgren (eds.), *Teleconferencing and Electronic Communications III.* Madison: University of Wisconsin, 1984.

Kirkpatrick, D. L. "Evaluation of Training." In R. Craig and L. Bittel (eds.), *Training and Development Handbook.* New York: McGraw-Hill, 1967.

Lazer, E., Elton, M., and Johnson, J. *The Teleconferencing Handbook: A Guide to Cost-Effective Communication.* New York: Knowledge Industry Publications, 1983.

Minnesota Extension Service. *Receiving Video Teleconferences: A Site Coordinator's Handbook.* St. Paul, Minn.: Teleconferencing Development Center, 1987.

Rice, R. *Human Communication Networking in Teleconferencing Environments.* Palo Alto, Calif.: Stanford University Press, 1982.

Shatzer, L. "Cost Effective Analysis of Teletraining." *Performance and Instruction,* 1987, *26* (9, 10), 48–51.

Short, J., Williams, E., and Christie, B. *Social Psychology of Telecommunications.* New York: Wiley, 1975.

Widner, D. *Teleguide: A Handbook on Video-Teleconferencing.* Washington, D.C.: Public Service Satellite Consortium, 1986.

*Linda Shatzer is a project manager for AT&T in the
Corporate Training Support Group. She manages an ongoing
teleconferencing series. In addition, she is a doctoral candidate
in the School of Communication and Information Science
at Rutgers University.*

*Staff development is different in the private and public/
nonprofit organizational worlds, although both sectors can
and do draw from each other. These differences are observable
in contextual influences, training for change, learning, and
reflective practice.*

Different Organizational Worlds: Patterns and Implications

Victoria J. Marsick

One cannot ignore differences between organizational worlds. The literature and practice of staff development is diverse and tailored to the unique needs of each group. It is difficult to generalize about what works, even if one is talking about similar organizations. Moreover, as Goldstein (1980, p. 231) notes in his thorough review of training literature, one must distinguish between fads and proved facts. This sourcebook is not sufficiently comprehensive for widespread generalizations. Nevertheless, this chapter revisits key themes identified in the Editor's Notes and brings together the collective wisdom of the contributors to this volume. The overarching question raised is what different organizational worlds have in common and what differences their unique contexts suggest.

The Private and Public/Nonprofit Sectors

One question raised in the Editor's Notes is the degree to which agencies in these two worlds are different. Some agencies outside the private sector are, wholly or in part, also driven by the need for profit. Hospitals are a prime example; their survival depends on innovative

V. J. Marsick (ed.). *Enhancing Staff Development in Diverse Settings.*
New Directions for Continuing Education, no. 38. San Francisco: Jossey-Bass, Summer 1988.

schemes for attracting clients. Profit is also crucial to most postsecondary education institutions. This volume shows that there are nevertheless some striking differences in staff development between these two organizational worlds.

Service Orientation. Public, nonprofit, and voluntary agencies are, by their self-designated missions, service-oriented—at least on paper. As such, they are oriented to the wishes of clients and may spend more time involving people in needs assessment, program design, and evaluation, which may affect staff development. Acebo and Watkins (Chapter Four) as well as Jacullo-Noto (Chapter Five), illustrate the role that staff can play in designing and implementing their own development plans and in keeping an eye both on the results of teaching and on complex systemic issues.

This difference may not always hold, since many businesses are also highly attuned to client and staff needs. Shatzer (Chapter Seven) demonstrates, for example, that her clients—other groups in the corporation—play a key role in the design of their own training. The M. Price Corporation, discussed in Chapter One, uses a service orientation to design learning for clients and staff; a key piece of this process is participation of the learner in design. Perhaps the common feature calling for participation has less to do with the profit-making status of the organization and more to do with the increasing professionalization of staff. As Benveniste (1987) points out, professionals are attracted to jobs because they provide autonomy and draw on expertise. Participation is not a matter of people-oriented versus task-oriented managerial style, but rather of involving people because of their knowledge and "communicating realistically instead of ritualistically" (p. 132).

Staff in agencies outside the private sector often perceive themselves as more people-oriented, perhaps because of this service orientation, even though motivation, personnel policies, and human relations may differ more by agency in either sector than across sectors. Pierce (Chapter Six) illustrates this when she notes that social service workers can be driven more by their own unmet needs than by the actual needs of clients. Moreover, some agencies must fight the image and reality of bureaucratic procedures, which increase distance between staff and clients and reduce the personal orientation. Volunteers, discussed by Rossing (Chapter Three), are an antidote to bureaucracy, since they bring to their jobs an idealism and a commitment not so easily influenced by the organizational norms, rewards, and punishments that may reduce people to numbers and forms to be filled out.

Nevertheless, the image espoused by various organizations in this sector is that people count more than profit and that, at the least, staff in these organizations will not deliberately trample on people for profit. Because of their people-centered missions, one might hypothesize that these organizations are more aware of the need for staff development. The examples in this volume both support and refute this hypothesis. Volunteers learn, but not necessarily by design. There is a high commitment in hospitals to training staff, but nurses are more valued for their technical expertise than for their capability to develop staff. Some colleges provide high-quality faculty development, but this is hardly the norm. Social service workers take on the development of others but often neglect their own growth. Still, staff in these organizations often have more leeway in deciding what they need to learn and meeting these needs in nontraditional ways, because staff development is less formalized.

Multiple Stakeholders. These organizations often involve a wider range of stakeholders than businesses do. Businesses have stockholders, who must be pleased with profits and who selectively exert influence on management, policies, and priorities, but the motivation of people interested in public, nonprofit, and voluntary groups spans a wider range: professional satisfaction, philanthropic concern, representation of interest groups, and political persuasions. Many of these groups are less hierarchical, more participatory, and more dependent on informal influence and persuasion to get things done. Others, such as hospitals and universities, are dominated by professional interest groups. Benveniste (1987, pp. 85–94) describes a variety of models by which professional organizations are governed: partnership, senior staff, dual governance, collegial, or bureaucratic. He notes, however, that all of them require a higher degree of participation if professionals are to be satisfied and effective.

Thus, while staff development's primary purpose may be individual and organizational growth, it is also used to ensure that multiple stakeholders buy into goals and programs. Staff development is thus a political process and, in some cases, a tool for the creation and maintenance of organizational norms, better known as corporate culture. Further, many stakeholders are not staff members but still need orientation and development for programs to run smoothly. Boards of these agencies, for example, often include interested members of the community, who help set policy and assist in fundraising. Different perspectives on issues may suggest education for board members, to resolve potential conflicts over the directions of the agency. Another set of stakeholders in both sectors is volunteers. Rossing (Chapter Three) discusses the reliance of many agencies on volunteers, who assist in fundraising activities, provide support services, and help implement programs. Volunteers need training and, like board members, can also encounter conflicts because of differences in perspective.

Qualitative Profit. Program success may be measured, wholly or in part, by qualitative changes that cannot be measured by statements of profit or returns on investments. Accountability and criteria for performance planning and appraisal are thus more ambiguous and often subject to more negotiation. Tolerance for ambiguity can strengthen staff development, as Marsick illustrates in Chapter One, where she discusses teamwork in today's organizations. In contrast, Pierce (Chapter Six) shows how this ambiguity can contribute to burnout in the absence of some system for clarifying goals, setting limits, and nurturing staff.

When organizations outside the private sector are tied less to short-run, quantitative gains, they may be more flexible and experimental in program initiatives, both for staff and for the clients served. Rossing (Chapter Three) quotes Langton (1982) when he suggests that the voluntary sector, in particular, can serve a modeling function by such experimentation. For example, staff may have a wider range of opportunities for career advancement or for professional and personal development. The model community college programs discussed by Acebo and Watkins (Chapter Four) illustrate the experimental nature of this kind of programming, while the teleconferencing series discussed by Shatzer (Chapter Seven) illustrates the need for the extensive resources of a large corporation to experiment with newer technologies for staff development.

Change

Questioning Assumptions. This volume began with a look at the changes that require new ways for individuals and organizations to learn. Key to this is questioning assumptions about individuals and organizations. Marsick (Chapter One) described a model for training private-sector managers to be international leaders that emphasizes just such questioning. Pierce (Chapter Six) talked about examining the paradox that emerges when trainers' own personal needs drive them to take responsibility for client change, instead of empowering clients to do this for themselves. Watkins (Chapter Two) uncovered taken-for-granted norms that lead staff developers to frustrate their own stated aims. Jacullo-Noto (Chapter Five) identified unexamined perceptions that university faculty and schoolteachers hold about one another and that interfere with learning and task accomplishment.

Critical thinking, a concern of teachers and educators for some time, is moving to center stage in the workplace, as discussed by this author elsewhere (Marsick, 1987, forthcoming) and as documented in this volume. Mezirow (1985) has developed a conceptual framework for critical thinking, on which Brookfield (1986, 1987) and this author have drawn, which begins with understanding the role played by questioning assumptions and values through three types of learning: instrumental, dialogic, and self-reflective. Instrumental learning is task-oriented; this author sees it as the primary focus and motive for workplace learning. Learning about tasks, however, requires the examination of socially created, consensual norms (most commonly reflected in the organization's culture), which is the focus of dialogic learning. Finally, individuals cannot change fundamentally without understanding how they must personally grow to undertake new tasks and cope with or change organizational norms. For example, the faculty discussed in Acebo and Watkins's chapter on community colleges must learn about adult development and learning and how they can best facilitate it, an instrumental task. In the process, they must work with other faculty and administrators to change the college's norms to reward this new behavior, and they must reflect on their own self-concepts as competent professional educators.

Revisiting Team Building. Change brings uncertainty, complexity, and nonroutine responses. As discussed in several chapters, response to change requires team learning across and within functions—not simply to collect information on which one person makes a decision, or to implement a decision made by one person, but to involve a wider variety of persons collegially in both setting and implementing goals. Rossing (Chapter Three) suggests that organizations outside the private sector may have models to do this more effectively, but the jury is still out on whether this is true. Many such organizations may even be more bureaucratic and hierarchical in nature than some large corporations. Pierce (Chapter Six) speaks to the cumbersome nature of bureaucracy in social service work and addresses ways in which managers can help staff deal with the burnout that results from an overload of social ills coupled with organizational conditions that have not kept up with change.

Other chapters speak to an awareness of the changing environment, although they do not always identify strategies that address these changes. Watkins (Chapter Two) notes the demands being placed on hospital staff to keep up with rapid technological and professional change. While her chapter primarily addresses nurse staff development, other health workers—from doctors to new categories of allied health professionals—face many challenges that call for continued learning. These challenges include AIDS, reimbursement based on diagnostic related groups that has implications for health care, and the use of computers for administrative and medical functions. Some learning needs are highly technical and individual, but others address the question of how individuals learn to work effectively as groups. While business struggles with new forms of teamwork, health professionals must revisit this issue. Health care training has often espoused a teamwork model, because patients need a single coordinated treatment plan, but teamwork has always been a struggle because of the hierarchical and status differentials among health care workers.

Action Research, Action Learning, and Action Science. Several chapters in this volume suggest that team building cannot be reduced to a set of exercises and techniques. Three concepts emerge that hold promise for team building, but they are tied to longer-range development strategies: action research, action learning, and action science. Marsick (Chapter One) and Watkins (Chapter Two) talk somewhat about action learning. Watkins draws specifically on action science, as advocated by Argyris, Schön, and their colleagues (Argyris and Schön, 1974; Argyris, Putnam, and Smith, 1985), and Jacullo-Noto (Chapter Five) illustrates action research. All three approaches employ some common methods.

Action research is frequently used in organizational development. Interventions of this kind involve collaborative diagnosis of problems and investigation of solutions by a consultant and individuals or groups in a system. Nevertheless, a drive toward action sometimes pushes these interventions toward problem solving, without sufficient attention to formulating the problem (a stage emphasized in action learning).

Action science differs from action research in several ways: Action science inevitably takes place through dialogue in a group, while action research can be undertaken by an individual with appropriate help from others, as needed. Action research is used to plan, elicit, and assess current or prospective behavior; action science analyzes completed social transactions—or those in progress, when the person acknowledges that usual responses are less than satisfactory—in order to influence future action. Both, however, have mutual inquiry and learning as their purpose.

Action research and action science, to some extent, frequently involve reliance on outside experts and consultants to help collect and interpret data on problems. At times, action research emphasizes problem solving, while action learning and action science both focus on problem formulation and difficulties encountered in trying to implement solutions. Action learning is typically undertaken by learners themselves, with the facilitator's role being that of a catalyst for reflection—that is, helping the actors to see a problem from multiple perspectives, slowing down the process of problem solving so that time is spent on learning how one best learns when situations are complex and ambiguous, digging into assumptions, assisting with group process, and helping individuals to gain insight related to individual professional concerns.

Despite their differences, all three strategies emphasize the value of working in teams to simultaneously deal with specific problems, and all use such problems for staff development that is directed at the individual and organizational norms that reinforce and encourage individual actions. These models capitalize on networks of self-directed learning professionals and create organizational learning systems responsive to shifts in the environment.

Learning and Reflection in Action

The contributors to this volume are highly attuned to learning, not just to models for "delivering" development. A consistent theme is learner-centeredness, which shows up in discussions of learning communities and of informal learning through experience. Informal learning suggests a strong focus in staff development on helping staff reflect in action, and on using such reflection as a key connection between formal and informal learning.

Creation of Learning Communities. While not losing the essentially instrumental focus of workplace learning, many contributors speak directly or indirectly of the creation of learning communities. The New York City Department of Sanitation, discussed in Chapter One, served as an example of the focus on learner-initiated problem identification and problem solving, which was transferred from the classroom to the job site. The models for action learning, action research, and action science created learning laboratories focused on real-life problems, both in project teams and in participants' regular jobs. Pierce (Chapter Six) suggests that managers can and should create learning communities as part of their supervisory responsibilities.

Acebo and Watkins (Chapter Four) also introduce the concept of organizational learning, which is relevant to a learning community but somewhat different from it. The important thing for most staff developers is the growth of individuals. Nevertheless, collective experience may transcend individual learning. People learn in groups and accept group norms that sometimes become unquestioned "wisdom" in the organizational culture. Staff developers could take the organization's learning more consciously into account in facilitating individual growth and could, through training, help individuals examine group-held norms.

Informal Learning Through Experience. Since many of these examples begin with the learner, they also start with people's experience, rather than with expert analysis of the tasks that the organization thinks people should perform. This is a departure from the prevailing "wisdom" of instructional systems design, but it may reflect a change in organizational needs and structures, as well as in the backgrounds and experiences of staff. The authors of this volume never abandon the notion of meeting organizational priorities, which employees implicitly and explicitly accept in their contracts, but they do suggest strategies to share responsibility for learning and make it more relevant. Formal programs, from training to development by such means as job rotation, are planned to meet needs, but needs are identified by the learner, in consultation with staff representing the institution's needs. The process of planning for development is negotiated, with more learner initiative, participation, and control.

Learning through experience is a concept that should be appealing to Americans rooted in pragmatism and organizational "can do." Despite a philosophy of self-reliance and an almost antiacademic strain in many businesses, managers and employees alike often seem to share a reverence for experts who will come into an organization and provide a "quick fix" to solve all woes. The contributors to this volume suggest longer-term, gradual processes that include, for example, totally informal, unplanned incidental learning (Watkins, Chapter Two), networks of learning relationships (Rossing, Chapter Three; Marsick, Chapter One), work design (Rossing, Chapter Three; Pierce, Chapter Six), learning journals (Rossing, Chapter Three), learning by study of one's own actions through action research (Jacullo-Noto, Chapter Five; Acebo and Watkins, Chapter Four), and action learning programs (Marsick, Chapter One; Watkins, Chapter Two) that build real-life experience into the training design.

Kolb's (1984) experiential learning theory is most widely used to interpret and plan for such activities. Kolb (pp. 1–19) discusses the thinking from which he draws—primarily Dewey's pragmatism, Lewin's Gestalt psychology and action research, and Piaget's developmental psychology. He also notes contributions to experiential learning theory from the therapeutic psychologists (Jung, Erikson, Rogers, Perls, and Maslow) and from the so-called radical educators, especially Freire and Illich. Kolb's work can be interpreted simplistically or used too prescriptively. Nevertheless, it does seem that learning through experience involves some kind of dialectical interaction between action and reflection and between direct experience and its abstract conceptualization. While the formulaic way in which Kolb has been interpreted may not accurately represent reality, this theory provides those who wish to be more learner-centered with a starting point for their practice.

An alternative to Kolb's theory is that of Cell (1984), whose conceptual framework is based on the work of Carl Rogers. Cell identifies four levels of change, each of which can involve experiential learning, and each of which builds on the previous level: response learning focused on behavior change, situation learning involving interpretation, transsituation learning, centered on autonomy, and transcendent learning leading to creativity (pp. 49–60). Cell brings to experiential learning theory a greater reliance on the way in which learners ascribe meaning to their experience, and a contrast among the multiple perspectives people can bring to their reality.

Reflective Practitioners. In this volume, the chapters by Marsick, Rossing, and Acebo and Watkins draw on some of the same philosophical roots as Kolb does when they discuss action learning or the work of Argyris and Schön. Reflection in action and action science can be traced, in part, to Dewey and Lewin. These strategies imply that staff development begins with the learner's regular habit of examining his or her own experience. Sometimes such reflection is simply directed at whether actions have produced desired results and, if not, why not. When events are surprising, or when there are paradoxes or contradictions between what one espouses and what one does, there is an opportunity to dig even more deeply for the underlying values, norms, and tacit personal rules that govern results. Staff development can be designed to develop the skills of reflective practice and to take advantage of the dilemmas, paradoxes, and problems faced by staff as they try to learn through experience.

Conclusion

Many questions still remain. For example, to what extent should the public, nonprofit, voluntary sector draw from the private sector for models of staff development? Citing Boyer's introduction to Eurich (1985), Houston (1986) draws implications for teacher education from a study of ten corporate and government training programs but warns, "While traditional educational institutions may learn much from the efficacy, flexibility and the clear sense of purpose in these private sector programs, copying them should be done judiciously" (p. 8). Houston underlines the very different mission of educational institutions, a point that must be raised for many organizations. Different missions require different modes of operation and attract staff whose motivations and reward systems may depart radically from those of staff in the private sector.

The private sector is often perceived as a leader in staff development, and there are lessons to be learned from its tighter focus and greater need for efficiency. Nevertheless, a question has also been raised about the appropriateness of some experimental practices that could be useful to the private sector. The public, nonprofit, voluntary sector has pioneered in a number of experimental learning approaches because of its scarce resources and the leeway some organizations have allowed staff for following divergent paths to meet learning needs. This volume has perhaps raised more questions than it has answered, but the contributors hope to have opened doors for further experimentation.

References

Argyris, C., Putnam, R., and Smith, D. M. *Action Science: Concepts, Methods, and Skills for Research and Intervention.* San Francisco: Jossey-Bass, 1985.

Argyris, C., and Schön, D. A. *Theory in Practice: Increasing Professional Effectiveness.* San Francisco: Jossey-Bass, 1974.

Benveniste, G. *Professionalizing the Organization: Reducing Bureaucracy to Enhance Effectiveness.* San Francisco: Jossey-Bass, 1987.

Brookfield, S. D. *Understanding and Facilitating Adult Learning: A Comprehensive Analysis of Principles and Effective Practices.* San Francisco: Jossey-Bass, 1986.

Brookfield, S. D. *Developing Critical Thinkers: Challenging Adults to Explore Alternative Ways of Thinking and Acting.* San Francisco: Jossey-Bass, 1987.

Cell, E. *Learning to Learn from Experience.* Albany: State University of New York Press, 1984.

Eurich, N. *Corporate Classrooms: The Learning Business.* Princeton, N.J.: The Carnegie Foundation for the Advancement of Teaching, 1985.

Goldstein, I. L. "Training in Work Organizations." *Annual Review of Psychology,* 1980, *31,* 229–272.

Houston, W. R. (ed.). *Mirros of Excellence: Reflections for Teacher Education from Training Programs in Ten Corporations and Agencies.* Reston, Va.: Association of Teacher Educators, 1986.

Kolb, D. A. *Experiential Learning.* Englewood Cliffs, N.J.: Prentice-Hall, 1984.

Langton, S. "The New Volunteerism." In J. Harmon (ed.), *Volunteerism in the Eighties.* Washington, D.C.: University Press of America, 1982.

Marsick, V. J. (ed.). *Learning in the Workplace.* Beckenham, Kent, England: Croom-Helm, 1987.

Marsick, V. J. "Learning in the Workplace: The Case for Reflectivity and Critical Reflectivity." *Adult Education Quarterly,* forthcoming.

Mezirow, J. D. "A Critical Theory of Self-Directed Learning." In S. Brookfield (ed.), *Self-Directed Learning: From Theory to Practice.* New Directions for Continuing Education, no. 25. San Francisco: Jossey-Bass, 1985.

Victoria J. Marsick, formerly director of staff training and development for UNICEF, is an assistant professor of adult education at Teachers College, Columbia University. Her special area of interest is workplace learning. She is a consultant to the private and the public sectors on staff development and training and is a member of the Institute for Leadership in International Management.

*The volume editor, with several associates, recommends sources
for further reading.*

Resources for Staff Developers

Victoria J. Marsick

Staff development is coming into its own as a professional field, but
capturing its literature is difficult, for many of the reasons discussed
in the Editor's Notes. This selective review begins with the general field
of training and development, highlights resources for professionals, and
concludes with literature that links training with informal learning.
Gloria Pierce, Boyd E. Rossing, and Karen Watkins contributed to the
selection and review of these resources.

General Resources

Overview. Literature providing an overview of training and development includes books and articles on the "state of the art." Two standard references in the first category are handbooks by Craig (1987) and
Nadler (1984). Craig's handbook is the third (revised) edition of what has
become a classic in the field. Its chapters cover almost every aspect of
training: its historical development as a field, learning theory, training
design, training management, and specialty areas. The chapters are written for the practitioner, but they refer to key pieces of literature. Nadler's
handbook covers similar topics and is also oriented to the practitioner.
Most overview books are addressed to the staff developer. Gloria Pierce
suggests Bellman (1985) for those interested in how the manager can

V. J. Marsick (ed.). *Enhancing Staff Development in Diverse Settings.*
New Directions for Continuing Education, no. 38. San Francisco: Jossey-Bass, Summer 1988.

develop staff. This book looks both at the skills needed by staff and at the tools available to managers to help staff develop these skills.

One of the key difficulties discussed in the Editor's Notes is getting a handle on the size and scope of the field. Carnevale and Goldstein (1983), Eurich (1985), and the American Society for Training and Development (ASTD) (1986) assist the reader in understanding this aspect of training for the private sector. Part of the difficulty in addressing size and scope is its ever-changing nature. Journal articles and reports supplement larger benchmark studies. As mentioned in the Editor's Notes, Lakewood Research conducts an annual survey of training, reported every October in *Training*.

Lusterman's (1985) report for the Conference Board also examines size and scope but focuses more on qualitative trends, illustrated by in-depth vignettes of training in different companies. *Training* publishes periodic supplements that address timely topics, and it covers current issues in its articles. Zemke (1986) provides a broad-based analysis of the factors that will affect staff development in the 1990s: external social forces, such as unionization, regulation, and litigation; changes in the work force itself; technology; and structural changes in organizations, such as downsizing, intrapreneuring, and entrepreneuring.

Professional Development Handbooks. Several recent books suggest strategies and resources for the trainer's own development. These books are especially valuable, because they typically include guides for self-development and lists of resources: books, periodicals, professional associations, films, and such technological aids as videos and computer software. Examples of these include Bard, Bell, Stephen, and Webster (1987) and McCullough (1987). The first book emphasizes the staff developer's own informal learning and includes chapters on learning from role models, mentors, and experience. The second book is tied to the ASTD competency study by McLagan (1983), a complete listing of functions, roles, and competencies needed by the training and development professional, and is more specifically behavioristic in its orientation than the book by Bard and others.

The ASTD competency study, currently being updated, provides a standard against which trainers can measure themselves. It reflects a common perspective in the field, described in a comprehensive literature review (Goldstein, 1980). The instructional systems-design approach evolved from psychology in the 1970s and has been adopted, almost to a fault, by many large private and public organizations (such as the military and government) wishing to impose criteria of accountability on trainers. This approach to training is typically competence-based, behavior-oriented, and designed to pass on the wisdom of experts. Many of the classic "how to" texts in training design are based on these instructional systems–design principles, although space is insufficient here to describe them.

Staff Development for Professionals

The contributors to this volume have identified a few specific resources for the development of health workers, educators, and volunteers. The literature on staff development in specific professional areas is rich in some ways and scanty in others. It crosses over into other topics, such as professional development and continuing professional education. Many of the professional associations have issued guidelines for continuing education, not only covering topics but also setting forth the number of credits that must be earned to maintain professional certification. The control function of such guidelines has spurred a general debate on whether continuing education should be mandatory.

Nurses and Health Workers. An example of professional guidelines is the set issued by the American Nursing Association (1978). This booklet defines staff development, sets forth a philosophy for continuing education, clarifies goals and roles, and discusses organization and administration. Karen Watkins recommends texts by O'Connor (1986) and Parker (1986). The O'Connor book is particularly comprehensive, spanning everything from instructional process to the management of educational programs for nurses. The orientation is practical, but it also provides a solid theoretical grounding. The book includes chapters on self-directed learning and professional development for staff developers. Parker's text is timely (if somewhat glib) and features numerous checklists, exercises, and session outlines. It mentions foundation chapters, manager development, and programs for all employees, including alcohol education and loss or grief counseling for caregivers. The final section describes alternative forms of staff development, such as films, fairs, and on-site college courses.

Educators. The literature on faculty and teacher development is vast and somewhat fragmented. The sources cited here are not particularly recent, but they capture relevant issues. Lieberman and Miller (1979) provide a conceptual framework for teacher education and school reform and illustrate it with case examples. They focus on *"staff development* instead of in-service or teacher education/training because it suggests a different approach to improvement, one that considers the effects of the whole school (the staff) on the individual (the teacher) and the necessity of long-term possibility (development)" (p. ix). Besides design issues, the collection considers many contextual factors: personal and professional, social, organizational, and political.

O'Banion's (1978) work is perhaps the most cited in commmunity college staff development. Because it was one of the few extended treatments on the topic, its prescriptive call is comprehensive, systematic, and consistent with the philosophy of the community college. O'Banion identifies common elements for staff development: assessment of resources, support, and need; a philosophical statement developed from "the ranks"; organization and staffing consistent with institutional size and prevailing practice; a wide variety of activities; appropriate incentives and rewards; adequate funding; and overall program evaluation. O'Banion (1977) had previously edited a sourcebook that described different strategies being used in staff development for faculty and administrators.

Linking Training with Informal Learning

Training literature deals primarily with organized education. This volume suggests that the lines between formal and informal learning are becoming blurred, as are distinctions between learning and other developmental strategies for growth.

Adult Learning Perspective. Authors grounded in adult learning use a theoretical base different from that of behavioral psychologists. Collins (1987) critiques the narrow focus of behaviorism and the way in which it reduces training to mechanical actions, without considering the meanings that people take from their lives and work. Kerrigan and Luke (1987), concerned with manager training in developing countries, provide a useful overview of learning on the job, action, training, and nonformal learning. Marsick (1987) has identified an emerging paradigm for workplace learning strategies, particularly self-directed learning, mentoring, and coaching. She also identifies training that can prepare people for more effective informal learning, can be founded on actual experience instead of expert-based information, and can create learning communities in organizations.

Long-Range Goals, Durations, and Payoffs. Strategies that emphasize learning rather than training tend to have long-range goals, durations, and payoffs. They are built around ongoing learning plans that incorporate a variety of activities. "Synergy," developed by Mouton and Blake (1984), is one type of long-range learning activity. Used successfully in both businesses and universities, synergogy is based on the shared-teaching concept. Four learning designs are described and illustrated in this volume: team effectiveness, team-member teaching, performance judging, and clarifying attitudes. Daloz (1986) offers additional ideas for individuals to benefit from teaching and mentoring relationships in courses, training programs, and other educational experiences. This book has much wisdom for those who guide adults through all phases of learning and help them overcome barriers encountered in the process.

Action learning, action science, and action research, discussed in several chapters in this volume, also illustrate a learning perspective. Action learning has a richer literature base in England than in America. Pedler (1983) is a good introduction to the topic. It includes a section on the conceptual framework for action learning, a range of applications (communities, schools, business, social services), a valuable guide to launching Action Learning programs, and a step-by-step action manual. The latest book on action science is by Argyris, Putnam, and Smith (1985). This book is comprehensive and oriented to spelling out procedures one can use to do action science, but those new to the subject might find Argyris (1985) easier going, because it provides extensive examples. Schön (1987), frequently cited in this volume, is probably even easier to understand. His book recapitulates his earlier thinking about reflection in action and illustrates it with examples drawn from many different work environments. Argyris, in contrast, focuses primarily on organization and management. Carr and Kemmis (1983) offer an excellent conceptual guide to action research for those engaged in teaching. Kemmis and McTaggart (1982) provide a practical guide for implementing these concepts.

Experience-Based Learning. Several contributors to this volume, have referred to Cell (1984) and Kolb (1984). Jarvis (1987) offers a valuable alternative perspective drawn from sociology. Keeton (Keeton and Associates, 1976) is a major contributor to experience-based learning in institutions and a force behind the Council for the Advancement of Experiential Learning (CAEL). The book cited here, an early classic, describes the relationship between experiential learning and higher education. Keeton and Tate (1978) define experiential learning, place it in historical context, and set forth a framework for understanding it. They distinguish between collegiate and noncollegiate experiential learning, and between sponsored and nonsponsored learning, but they focus primarily on postsecondary institutions. Byrne and Wolfe (1980) edited a volume of conceptual and practical articles on experiential program design in formal institutions of professional development. These conceptual articles highlight the work of Kolb and Keeton, although one chapter by Bill Joiner is more influenced by action science. Lewis (1986) draws conceptually on Kolb's work and provides many excellent examples of how experience-based learning can be achieved.

References

American Nursing Association. *Guidelines for Staff Development.* Kansas City, Mo.: American Nursing Association, 1978.

American Society for Training and Development. *Serving the New Corporation.* Alexandria, Va.: ASTD Press, 1986.

Argyris, C. *Strategy, Change, and Defensive Routines.* Cambridge, Mass.: Pitman, 1985.

Argyris, C., Putnam, R., and Smith, D. M. *Action Science: Concepts, Methods, and Skills for Research and Intervention.* San Francisco: Jossey-Bass, 1985.

Bard, R., Bell, C., Stephen, L., and Webster, L. *The Trainer's Professional Development Handbook.* San Francisco: Jossey-Bass, 1987.

Bellman, G. *The Quest for Staff Leadership.* Glenview, Ill.: Scott, Foresman, 1985.

Byrne, E. T., and Wolfe, D. E. (eds.). *Developing Experiential Learning Programs for Professional Education.* New Directions for Experiential Learning, no. 8. San Francisco: Jossey-Bass, 1980.

Carnevale, A. P., and Goldstein, H. *Employee Training: Its Changing Role and an Analysis of New Data.* Washington, D.C.: ASTD Press, 1983.

Carr, W., and Kemmis, S. *Becoming Critical: Knowing Through Action Research.* Victoria, Australia: Deakin University Press, 1983.

Cell, E. *Learning to Learn from Experience.* Albany: State University of New York Press, 1984.

Collins, M. *Competence in Adult Education: A New Perspective.* New York: University Press of America, 1987.

Craig, R. L. (ed.). *Training and Development Handbook: A Guide to Human Resource Development.* 3rd ed. New York: McGraw-Hill, 1987.

Daloz, L. A. *Effective Teaching and Mentoring: Realizing the Transformational Power of Adult Learning Experience.* San Francisco: Jossey-Bass, 1986.

Eurich, N. *Corporate Classrooms: The Learning Business.* Princeton, N.J.: The Carnegie Foundation for the Advancement of Teaching, 1985.

Goldstein, I. L. "Training in Work Organizations." *Annual Review of Psychology,* 1980, *31,* 229–272.

Jarvis, P. *Adult Learning in the Social Context.* London: Croom-Helm, 1987.

Keeton, M. T., and Associates. *Experiential Learning: Rationale, Characteristics, and Assessment.* San Francisco: Jossey-Bass, 1976.

Keeton, M. T., and Tate, P. J. (eds.). *Learning by Experience: What, Why, How.* New Directions for Experiential Learning, no. 1. San Francisco: Jossey-Bass, 1978.

Kemmis, S., and McTaggart, R. *The Action Research Planner.* Victoria, Australia: Deakin University Press, 1982.

Kerrigan, J. E., and Luke, J. S. *Management Training Strategies for Developing Countries.* Boulder, Colo.: Lynne Rienner, 1987.

Kolb, D. A. *Experiential Learning.* Englewood Cliffs, N.J.: Prentice-Hall, 1984.

Lewis, L. H. (ed.). *Experiential and Simulation Techniques for Teaching Adults.* New Directions for Continuing Education, no. 30. San Francisco: Jossey-Bass, 1986.

Lieberman, A., and Miller, L. *Staff Development: New Demands, New Realities, New Perspectives.* New York: Teachers College Press, 1979.

Lusterman, S. *Trends in Corporate Education and Training.* New York: The Conference Board, 1985.

McCullough, R. C. *Planning Your Professional Development in Human Resources Development.* Alexandria, Va.: ASTD Press, 1987.

McLagan, P. *Models for Excellence: The Conclusions and Recommendations of the ASTD Training and Development Competency Study.* Alexandria, Va.: ASTD Press, 1983.

Marsick, V. J. (ed.). *Learning in the Workplace.* Beckenham, Kent, England: Croom-Helm, 1987.

Mouton, J. S., and Blake, R. R. *Synergogy: A New Strategy for Education, Training, and Development.* San Francisco: Jossey-Bass, 1984.

Nadler, L. (ed.). *The Handbook of Human Resource Development.* New York: Wiley, 1984.

O'Banion, T. (ed.). *Developing Staff Potential.* New Directions for Community Colleges, no. 19. San Francisco: Jossey-Bass, 1977.

O'Banion, T. *Organizing Staff Development Programs That Work.* Washington, D.C.: American Association of Community and Junior Colleges, 1978.

O'Connor, A. *Nursing Staff Development and Continuing Education.* Boston: Little, Brown, 1986.

Parker, B. *Health Care Education: A Guide to Staff Development.* East Norwalk, Conn.: Appleton-Century-Crofts, 1986.

Pedler, M. (ed.). *Action Learning in Practice.* Aldershot, Hants, England: Gower, 1983.

Schön, D. A. *Educating the Reflective Practitioner: Toward a New Design for Teaching and Learning in the Professions.* San Francisco: Jossey-Bass, 1987.

Zemke, R. "Training in the 90's." *Training,* 1986, *23* (1), 36–44.

Victoria J. Marsick, formerly director of staff training and development for UNICEF, is an assistant professor of adult education at Teachers College, Columbia University. Her special area of interest is workplace learning. She is a consultant to the private and the public sectors on staff development and training and is a member of the Institute for Leadership in International Management.

Index